Franz Sauter
Tonal Music

Franz Sauter

Tonal Music

Anatomy of the Musical Aesthetics

Translated by Saša Šarenac

Bibliographic information published by the Deutsche Nationalbibliothek
The Deutsche Nationalbibliothek lists this publication in the Deutsche
Nationalbibliografie; detailed bibliographic data are available on the
Internet at http://dnb.dnb.de.

First English edition: 2020
First German edition: 2000, Title: Die tonale Musik

ISBN: 9783750434592

Contents

III. Melodics

6. Aesthetics of Scale Degree Relations

7. Counterpoint

8. Aesthetics of the Motiv

"For some time, efforts have been made to explain our music theoretically. Still we have to admit to ourselves that we do not really have a true system ... The musical Galilei, we are still missing ..." (Heinrich Josef Vincent, *Die Einheit in der Tonwelt*, Leipzig 1862, preface)

"... a real theory, a scientifically founded music theory that deserves its name ... does not yet exist, however." (Martin Vogel, *Die Lehre von den Tonbeziehungen*, Bonn 1975, p. 358)

Preface

Harmony, rhythm, and melody are the three basic features of our present-day music that are usually mentioned in one breath. No one would seriously assert that they only happen to meet in music by chance. Nevertheless, there is to date no scientific representation of the music which demonstrates that these three aesthetic characteristics necessarily cohere and which develops the musical concepts accordingly. Instead, music theory juxtaposes harmony, rhythm, and melody as subfields without revealing any inner connection. This is symptomatic of a state of musicology to which still applies what was already noted in the 19th century about the efforts to establish its theoretical foundation:

"All attempts of this kind have, up to now, not been able to create a really tenable scientific-musical system according to which all phenomena in the musical field are presented to be always necessary consequences of one basic principle ... But what is laid down in musical textbooks with scientific justification has so far proved a failure, partly ... because it was just as little able to create a self-contained system with undoubted conclusions, partly because, as a fantastic construction, it lacked any scientific basis." [1]

The present book on the tonal music and the laws of its beauty emerged from a project initiated in 1980 to overcome the deficiency mentioned by Richter and to present the basic musical forms systematically and coherently. The reader can now be informed about what harmonic, rhythmic, and melodic structures have in common, how they differ, and how they are connected internally. The fact that such an analysis also yields some surprising results lies in the nature of a project that did not want to settle for the previous state of knowledge in musicology. The reader is therefore cordially invited to verify the validity of a whole series of unfamiliar findings and conclusions.

---

[1] Ernst Friedrich Richter, *Lehrbuch der Harmonie*, Leipzig 1886, preface to the first edition (1853).

9

I. Harmonics

1. Consonance

a) Harmony of the Basic Consonance

Tonal music is music on a harmonic basis. The key to its aesthetics lies in the analysis of the major and minor triads, the basic sound forms of the tonal music. In the progress of the analysis, it will become apparent how any harmony, rhythm, and melody of the tonal music is built upon the harmony of these two sound figures.

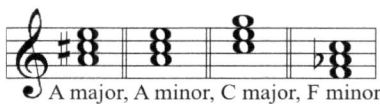

A major, A minor, C major, F minor

Major and minor triads

Major and minor triads are triads whose tones harmonise with each other. What characterises these triads are the *relations* between the three tones called the root, third, and fifth. Only *because of and within these relations*, musical tones are defined as a root, third, and fifth. It is therefore quite appropriate to name the *tones* third and fifth after their *relation* to the root, which in turn would not be a root tone without these relations.

The relation between the tones third and fifth is again a third. Each major or minor triad contains in its basic form a major and a minor third, which complete each other to form a fifth. The major triad has the major third in the bottom part, the minor triad has it on top. Both sound forms have something in common: a specific harmony, which is called consonance. The essence of this harmony shall now be explained.

The harmony of the major and minor triads is obviously related to the frequency ratios that are characteristic of these sound forms:

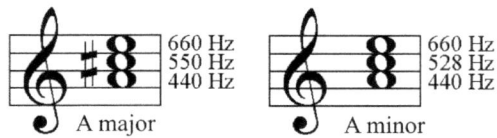

Tone frequencies of two triads

The frequency ratios of these triads are:

Fifth:	660 Hz : 440 Hz		= **3:2**
Major third:	550 Hz : 440 Hz	= 660 Hz : 528 Hz	= **5:4**
Minor third:	660 Hz : 550 Hz	= 528 Hz : 440 Hz	= **6:5**

The mathematical ratios between the frequencies of harmonising tones are of interest in instrument making, where these proportions have to be considered with regard to the dimensions of resonating cavities or strings. An organ pipe, for example, has to be the longer the lower its tone and the smaller therefore the related tone frequency. The frets on a guitar neck must be positioned in such a way that, for example, the tones of a major triad can be played one after the other on a single string, which presupposes that the vibrating string parts have the frequency ratio 4:5:6. Since the lengths of vibrating string parts are inversely proportional to the number of vibrations per second, the numerical ratios that are decisive for the harmonising tones have a clear appearance. It is therefore not surprising that the proportion 2:3 as a length ratio of string parts was known long before the knowledge of tone frequencies, namely, already in ancient times.

However, the quantitative relations observable in connection with major and minor triads (the proportions 3:2, 5:4, and 6:5) merely indicate the *external* relations between the tone frequencies. The question of the harmonic character of these sound relations is thereby in no way answered. Harmony, as a characterisation of what is perceived during the sounding of major and minor triads, means, namely, an *inner* relation of the tones respectively sounding together: a relation in which the musical tones go well together.

The basis for the fact that contents of perception go well together – and, by the way, that is what any aesthetics is all about – lies always in the properties of these things. In the case of major and minor triads, it is obviously the tones themselves that have something about themselves that makes them go well together. This property of the musical tones has therefore to be examined more closely.

A tone with a frequency of 500 Hz oscillates by definition 500 times per second, that is, once every two milliseconds. On an oscillograph, these oscillations are displayed, for example, as follows:

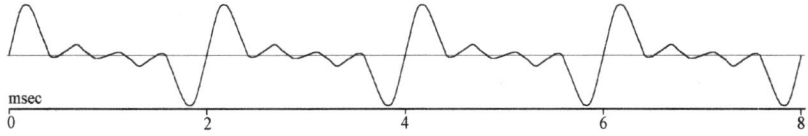

Four oscillations of a tone of 500 Hz

As the physicist and mathematician Jean Baptiste Fourier has generally demonstrated, regular oscillations are composed of simple sine oscillations. In music, these are referred to as partial tones of a musical tone.[1] A single vibration of the above form consists of four partial tones:

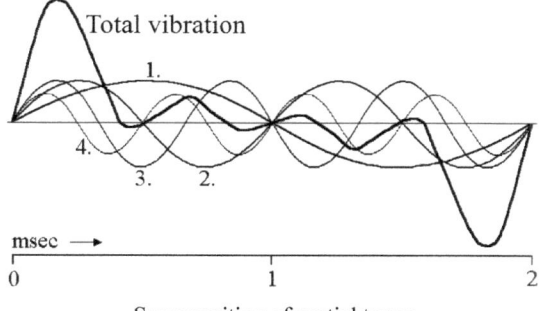

Superposition of partial tones

While the first partial tone executes *one* oscillation, the second does *two*, the third *three*, and the fourth *four* vibrations. Accordingly, the partial tones vibrate at the basic frequency, double frequency, triple and quadruple frequency. The linear superposition of these oscillations results in a total vibration of the displayed form.

The illustration shows only a simple example. Musical tones normally consist of many more partial tones so that even the fifth, sixth, seventh etc. partial tones are contained in the sound. The sound spectrum of a tone contains a whole series of partial tones that are integer multiples of the basic vibration. Individual partial tones can vibrate more or less powerfully so that different waveforms are the result, which are perceived as specific timbres and acoustic colours. With the use of the Fourier analysis, it can be determined how strongly each single partial tone oscillates in the sound of a musical tone. This gives the characteristic sound spectrum, in which every partial oscillation is displayed with its frequency and volume.

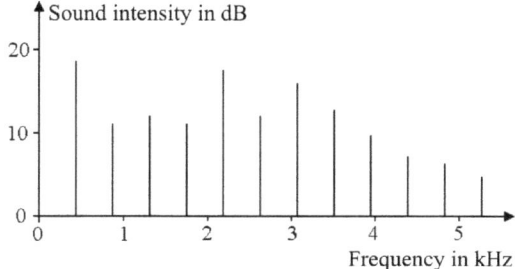

Sound spectrum of a violin tone of 440 Hz

---

[1] In a physical sense, partial tones are sine waves. In this regard, one speaks of "harmonic oscillations" or "harmonic motions". The physical attribute "harmonic" and the designation of partial tones as "harmonics" have nothing to do with harmony in an aesthetic sense.

The sound of a tone results from its inner composition. The fact that a tone always has a sound character is, on the one hand, quite natural because mechanical oscillations have a more or less pronounced sound spectrum, simply for physical reasons. On the other hand, the fact that musical tones are *rich* in partial tones is not a mere natural phenomenon, because it is the result of a sophisticated instrument making. The sonority of the tones is achieved by various techniques: by the positioning of the violin bow when stroking the strings, by resonance bodies, by octave couplers of an organ, etc. The musical sound is cultivated for its own sake; it is designed as an object of enjoyment.

The quality of the tones by which they are predestined to harmonise can thus be summarised as follows: It is a matter of *sonorous* tones insofar as they are composed of a whole series of partial tones. Obviously, the harmony between the tones does not depend on their particular timbre and sound colour. The sonorous tone can therefore be represented schematically, by abstracting from the sonic intensity of the individual partial tones:

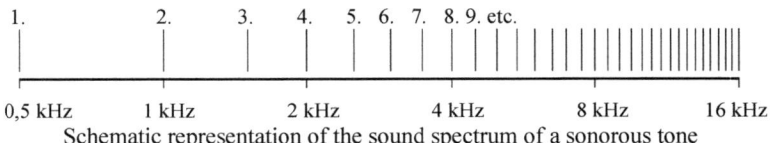

Schematic representation of the sound spectrum of a sonorous tone

In this illustration, the frequencies are scaled logarithmically. This representation has the advantage that equal frequency ratios appear as equal distances, as comes closest to the perspective of musicians who are familiar with this view due to the musical notation, the piano keyboard, etc.

By comparing the sound spectra of two tones that have the frequency ratio 3:2, one can see that every second partial tone of the higher tone oscillates at the same frequency as every third partial tone of the lower tone.

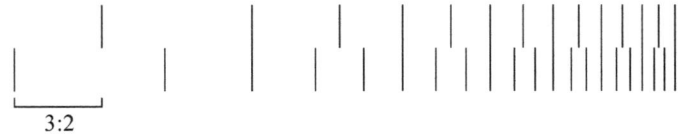

Consonance schema of the fifth

The two sonorous tones have thus coinciding partial tones. In the sounding-together of the tones, the oscillations of their common partial tones overlap to form a *single* partial oscillation in each case, in which even the Fourier analysis cannot indicate to which tone belongs which share in the sound intensity of a partial tone. Only the schematic separation of the tones can reveal the different origin of the partial tone in question.

Now it becomes apparent in what way both of the tones of a fifth harmonise: They match as sonorous tones, based on an accordance of their sound parts. This effect shall be called *basic consonance*.[1]

As said before, the harmony in the sounding-together of the sonorous tones is in any case independent of their specific timbre and acoustic colour. In the sound spectrum of tones, individual partial oscillations can therefore be completely absent without this diminishing the effect of the consonance. This applies, for example, to the clarinet, whose tones do not have even-numbered partials in its sound spectrum. The coincidence of partial tones also includes the case where a partial oscillation of a tone lies on a frequency that is a multiple of the basic frequency of another tone. That this other tone lacks a partial tone at the concerning position, is no reason for the ear to ignore the principle assignment of partial vibrations to a basic frequency. The detectable vibration has therefore partial tone character for both tones, even if it has its origin in only one of the tones. Basic consonance is therefore, strictly speaking, the harmony of a sound combination in which vibrations occur that have partial tone character for both of the sounding together tones alike.

Experiments have shown that, after an adaption phase, test persons can consider relations between sinus tones – even if they are offered separately for each ear through headphones – to be consonances. Testers and test persons have the freedom to call acoustic phenomena consonances if they remind them of consonances, although individual sinus tones cannot harmonise at all. Such experiments do not disprove the concept of the consonance, but are at most evidence for the susceptibility of the perception for illusions, which can come about under the participation of other mental capacities like memory, imagination, mind, and interest.[2]

When schemata of different consonances are compared, one can see that the extent of the coincidence of partial tones can be expressed by the ratio of the total vibrations of the tones: In the case of the fifth, the frequency ratio 3:2 equals a harmony in which every *second* partial tone of the one tone coincides with every *third* one of the other tone. The frequency ratio of the major third (5:4) corre-

---

[1] Husmann formulated this realisation still most clearly: *"Since for the consonance the coincidence of common overtones would thus be responsible, the author has described his theory as the* coincidence theory *of the consonance ... It is the greater harmony of the, above the root tones rising, overtone structure of intervals with simple vibration ratios, which makes them appear consonant ..."* (Heinrich Husmann, *Einführung in die Musikwissenschaft*, Heidelberg 1958, pp. 134 f.)

[2] Husmann lets himself be theoretically confused by such experiments and concedes consonance in the relation of mere sine oscillations: *"Since at the binaural experiments, aside from the overtones, only the primary tones themselves are present, the assumption cannot be excluded that the consonance is also already founded in the primary tones alone ..."* (Ibid., p. 135). More about Husmann's theory of the consonance in: Franz Sauter, *Die Musikwissenschaft in Forschung und Lehre. Kritik einer bürgerlichen Wissenschaft*, Norderstedt 2010, chapter 3.

sponds to a harmony in which every *fifth* partial tone of the one tone coincides with every *fourth* one of the other tone.

Consonance schema of a major third

The conspicuous numerical proportions, which are characteristic for harmonic sound combinations and which can be read off accordingly from the length ratios of vibrating strings or air columns, have therefore their reason in the sound architecture of the tones. The proportions that can be observed in the *external* tone relations are the necessary manifestation of the *inner* relations that the sonorous tones have to each other because of their internal structure. The essence of the harmony lies definitely not in the *numerical ratios*, but in the *going well together* of the tones that is based on their sound character.

The difference in the degree of the harmony, which can be seen at the consonance schemata, is intuitively felt when comparing tone ratios acoustically. Since the weaker or stronger harmony of the sounding-together tones is related to the proportion of their frequencies, which is easily determinable, the illusion arises as if the frequency ratios themselves have a harmonic character. The theoretical deepening of this confusion consequently ends up in number mysticism, which subscribes to the believe that the harmony that is inherent to the sounding-together of the tones is a property of the associated external numerical proportions.

The consonance of the fifth and thirds is summarized in the harmony of the major or minor triad:

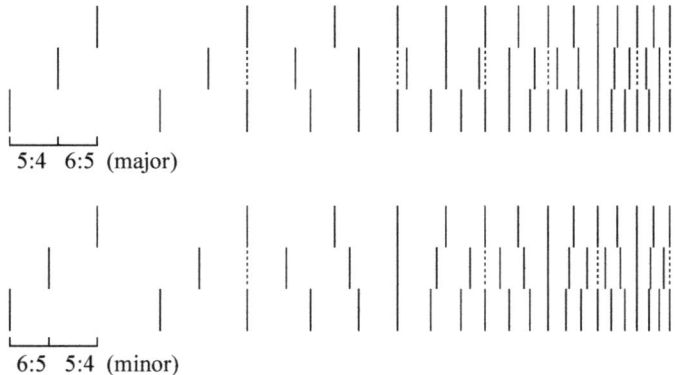

Consonance schemata of a major and minor triad

The mere summing-up of the consonances to a triad intensifies the effect of the basic consonance. The reason for this is that the combination of two consonances automatically includes a third consonance, whose harmony thus comes in addition 'for free'. This is equally true for major and minor triads. However, the schematic representation of their consonance also shows a specific difference in the harmonic structure of the major and minor triads.

In case of the major triad, the coincidences of partial tones extend over more frequencies than in case of the minor triad. This is, for one thing, due to the fact that these coincidences are more widely dispersed in the major triad, whereas, in the minor triad, they are more concentrated on frequencies where all three tones have common partial oscillations. For another, there is more accordance in total in the major triad. Within the bandwidth illustrated above, the major triad has twelve times common partial oscillations, whereas the minor triad shows only ten such coincidences. This harmonic difference is the reason why musicians are able to intuitively distinguish major and minor triads on the basis of their sound. Also, the greater consonance of the major triad is noticeable when compared acoustically.

The consonant triad perfects the principle of the harmony that is contained in its components, the consonant dyads (fifth and thirds). It follows from this that the actual harmonic potency of the fifth and the thirds comes into effect in their determination as subordinate moments in the harmony of the consonant triads. Their harmonic role in tonal music is entirely in accordance with this: The fifth is a sound that is always defined by the sound relations of major and minor triads; it is divided in one way or another by thirds. Likewise, major and minor thirds are not autonomous harmonies, but are in each case components of either a major or a minor triad.

b) Compound Consonance

The musician distinguishes the basic form of a major and minor triad from the other forms in which individual tones are shifted to sound one or more octaves higher or lower or in which tones are supplemented by accordingly shifted tones. This distinction is determining for the practical handling of the harmonies in tonal music.

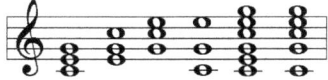

Basic form, inversions and extended forms of a C major triad

All of these sound shapes are named C major, even though they are quite different: Tones of varying numbers and positions sound together in it. On the other hand, it is not a matter of a random name equivalence, as is the case with persons, for example, who are all called Paul. Rather, it is a matter of an *appropriate* subsumption of sounds under a collective term. The use of the term 'C major triad' in the above example shows that musicians consider an equal treatment of these sounds as reasonable. They therefore abstract from the differences of these sounds; and they do rightly so: They take into account that an actual commonality of these sounds do exist. But *what* is it that is being abstracted from and *what* is the commonality of all these sound shapes?

First of all, all of these chords sound very similar. In this respect, the commonality of the forms of a major or minor triad is their belonging to a family of sounds that differ only slightly when listening to. However, this similarity, which the musician intuitively grasps, lies on the level of the immediate appearance and does not justify a conceptual abstraction which can last against errors and misperceptions. In biology, for example, the external similarity of animal species is a starting point for a classification, but it does not necessarily reveal the animal's true nature. Accordingly, whales are, despite all appearances, not fish but mammals.

When musicians identify a major or minor triad independently of its particular form, they abstract from a difference that in fact only represents a harmonic nuance. It is a matter of that difference that makes itself felt when a tone within a sound combination is substituted or supplemented by another tone that lies one or more octaves higher or lower. Obviously, the sound relation of the octave does not create by itself any significant harmonic differences.

2:1

Consonance schema of the octave

Tones sounding together in an octave ratio appear as a dyad with an unsurpassable consonance because the complete sound of the upper tone coincides with half the sound of the lower tone. What presents itself as a similarity in the harmonic comparison of the different shapes of a triad is the same thing that appears as an extra strong harmony in the perception of the octave: the accordance of the sounds in regard to the frequencies of their partial tones. In realising major and minor triads and, accordingly, in the entire world of harmony that is based on major and minor triads, one thus *abstracts* from the harmony of the octave.

However, the neglect of the octave when determining major and minor triads is, in substance, not a disregard of the octave, but its consideration. The musical treatment of the octave fully corresponds to its harmonic property. That the octave causes only a negligible harmonic difference is only the flip side of a superlative of the consonance. The insignificance of the octave in a sphere, where it is about the harmonic identity of the sounds, is the form in which its absolutely dominant position in the harmonics of the tonal music comes into its own. The octave is therefore a substantial part of the consonant dyads which in their combination to major or minor triads perfect the principle of the consonance.

What applies to the major and minor triads as a whole, also applies to their components – the thirds and fifths. These, too, are to be understood abstractly and grasped in accordance with their harmonic essence against their specific manifestations:

Inversion of the fifth and of the major third

The fourth (4:3) is harmonically the same as the fifth (3:2), and the minor sixth (8:5) is the same as the major third (5:4), as Jean-Philippe Rameau already stated.[1] The reason is obviously the harmony of the octave, which determines the sound image of the fourth and sixth. The harmony of the in such a way modified shapes of the fifth and thirds shall be called *compound consonance*.

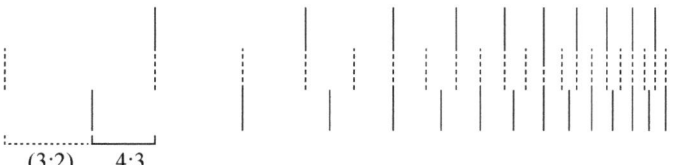

The fourth as a compound consonance

The dashed lines in the consonance schema of the fourth indicate an imaginary tone that forms an octave along with the upper tone of the fourth, and a fifth along with the lower tone. These lines illustrate the intermediate step in the harmonic constitution of a fourth. The harmony of the fourth is not reduced to the immediate coincidence of the partials in this sound combination, but unites the harmony of the octave and fifth:

$$4:3 = (2:3) \cdot (2:1)$$

The practical equation of the various forms of major and minor sounds thus allows a conclusion to be drawn on the specific capacity of the musical perception to intuitively break down sound relations into their simple components.

If one wanted to adequately express what the fourth is and what it represents for the perception, then one could write the frequency ratio in the following form: $2^2:3$. But this is merely a mathematical illustration of the compound consonance at the level of its external frequency ratios. At this level, the consonance cannot be grasped anyway, and the formula

$$3:2 = 4:3$$

appears as a mathematical nonsense. Accordingly, the difference between the basic and compound consonance appears to be erased in the form of the frequen-

---

[1] Rameau thus calls the fourth the "shadow image" (l'ombre) of the fifth, following an expression of Descartes (Cf. Jean-Philippe Rameau, *Traité de l'harmonie réduite à ses principes naturels*, Paris 1722, p. 11).

cy ratios. Theorists who confuse the outward appearance of the harmonies with their essence locate the fourth harmonically between the fifth and the third because they are fascinated and dazzled by the mathematical series

$$2:1, \quad 3:2, \quad 4:3, \quad 5:4, \quad 6:5.$$

If the fifth and fourth are presented in such a series, then the difference in their kind of consonance is ignored as well as the commonality in their abstract harmonic essence. It is then not surprising that such a theory construction gets into trouble when, at first, it misinterprets the consonance as a relation of small numbers, to then speculate and wonder whether the relation 16:5 (a variant of the major third) can be a consonance or not.[1]

The abstract identity of the consonant sounds is finally reflected by the tones of which they consist:

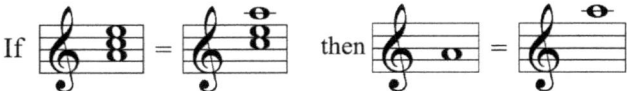

The tones that sound together in a ratio of 2:1 are identical because and insofar it is abstracted from their insignificant contribution to the harmonic differentiation in all sound combinations. Thus, in addition to the concrete tone appears the tone in its abstract definition so that because of this double meaning of the term tone it can be said that the octave is a harmonic relation between identical tones. It is therefore quite consistent and appropriate if the respective tones are given the same name.[2]

---

[1] An example of this speculation: *"The tones of consonant sounds stand in simple frequency proportions to each other. However, the consonance phenomenon can neither be clearly explained mathematically nor physically."* (Gerhard Kwiatkowski et al. (eds.), *Meyers kleines Lexikon Musik*, Mannheim et al. 1986, p.186). The theorists have blocked their path to a *musical* explanation of the consonance by their preference for *extra-musical* patterns of interpretation.

[2] Jean-Phillipe Rameau already noticed that the same naming of different tones reflects an objective harmonic fact. With such terms as "inversion", "root tone" etc., he coined the generally accepted terminology used today, which takes this discovery into account. However, he did not realise the abstraction on the basis of which it makes sense to speak of identical tones in the case of the octave. Likewise, he overlooked the underlying harmony (the fitting-together) of the tones because he did not doubt the (up to the present day) popular idea of a harmony that is inherent to the numerical proportions. In the ratio of 2:1, he therefore sought to find a property that would make the identity of the tones plausible: *"La proportion du tout à sa moitié, ou de la moitié au tout est si naturelle, qu' elle se conçoit d' abord; ce qui doit nous prévenir en faveur de l'Octave, dont la raison est comme 1. à 2. l'Unité est le principe des nombres, & 2. en est le premier, se trouvant un grand rapport entre ces deux Epithetes, Principe & Premier, dont l'application est tres-juste. Aussi dans la pratique, l'Octave n'est distinguée que sous le nom de réplique;..."* (Rameau, *Traité de l'harmonie réduite à ses principes naturels*, p. 6)

The musician usually imagines the matter the other way round: The identity of two harmonies seems logical to him insofar as the harmonies consist of the same tones. And that these tones are equal is not familiar to him as a harmonic abstraction, but by the names under which the tones were introduced to him. That works very well in practice. Why racking one's brain over the absurdity that language rules are supposed to have an effect on the identity of harmonies?

The abstract definition of the tones is also reflected in the designation of the tones of major and minor triads: Root tone, third, and fifth are, regardless of their respective octave position, the only components of these sounds, which exactly therefore are consonant *triads* in the abstract sense, and not only in the basic form analysed at the beginning, but in all other forms as well. The lowest tone of a chord is therefore not the same as its root tone. This also applies to the harmonic components of the triads: The fourth has its root tone on top, that is, it is the fifth turned upside-down.

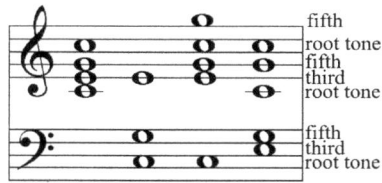

Root tone, third and fifth in C major triads

c) Theories About Major and Minor Triads

Gioseffo Zarlino was the first one to express the opinion that major and minor triads are the basic shapes of the harmonics. He opposed the then usual treatment of the thirds as "imperfect" sound combinations. This treatment was based on the Pythagorean tuning, which deduces all tone relations from fifths so that the frequency ratio of the major third does not have the numeric value of

$$5:4 \ = \ 1.25$$

but

$$81:64 \ = \ 1.265625$$

In order to prove the harmonic character of major and minor triads, however, he lacked the necessary fundamentals, namely the knowledge about the inner structure of the tones. Actually, he should have realised that he was not capable of explaining the harmonic principle of the consonance. Nevertheless, he realised that consonant tone relations can be demonstrated by dividing a vibrating string by 2, 3, 4, 5, and 6. As a matter of fact, this results in the oscillation ratios of the octave, fifth, fourth, and thirds. This induced Zarlino to assume that the reason for the correlation between the consonance and the observed numerical proportions lies in a specialty of the number six. To that end he applied two traditional thought patterns of the mystical numerology:

First, he claims to know a mathematical quality of the number six, which he calls 'perfect'. He, thereby, creatively complements the presentation of the known types of numbers like prime numbers etc.: *"Perfect numbers are those which can be added up from their parts..."* [1] In order to make the assumed perfection clear, he says that the number six has *"a certain measure whereby nothing is too much and nothing too little."* [2]

Second, he calls attention to the role of the number six in many important contexts. This starts in the Holy Scriptures right off with the story of creation and is then soon broken off for good reasons: *"It would take a long time to recount all the things in detail that come to a completion with the number six."* [3]

The effort to prove specific tone relations to be necessary manifestations of the consonance never gets to the essence of the consonance in this way because it does not thematise *its* property, but instead the property of a number. As an explanation of major and minor triads, it is offered that they be attested by laws that are supposed to prevail *regardless* of any music. This is an interpretation within the framework of a worldview.

200 years later, when it was known that the musical tones consist of partial tones, nothing more would have stood in the way of exploring the consonance. In fact, the major and minor triads were associated with partial tones, but merely as a continuation of the endeavour to substantiate the aesthetic quality of these triads with outside existing phenomena. The inner structure of the tones serves from now on in speculative music theory as a model, as a pattern of nature, to which harmony is imitated. The appeal of this model lies in its character as an undoubted and experimentally verifiable natural phenomenon. This is supposed to guarantee a harmonic quality separately from the examined harmonies.

Very common is the interpretation of the major triad as a replication of the fourth, fifth, and sixth partial tones. In the case of the minor triad, one discovers either a direct model that is given in the relation of the 10th, 12th, and 15th partial tones; or one believes that only dyads are "naturally" prefigured in the overtone series, namely the thirds, from which major and minor triads are then "artificially" put together; or one imagines a reverse "undertone series", which, however, is not detectable in nature, but instead fits well into the imagination of a *"truth of nature of the dual harmony principle ..."*. [4] The speculative musicology can draw on an inexhaustible pluralism of such theories, which classify themselves within a factional dispute between monists and dualists and which are

---

[1] Gioseffo Zarlino, *Theorie des Tonsystems. Das erste und zweite Buch der Istituzioni harmoniche (1573)*, trans. Michael Fend, Frankfurt am Main 1989, p. 79.

[2] Ibid., p. 84.

[3] Ibid., p. 85.

[4] Hugo Riemann, *Handbuch der Harmonielehre*, Leipzig 1918, p. 214.

supported in this classification by an academic reporting system that is rather striving for a rubrication of theories than for a scientific explanation.[1]

The contrasts of the theories on major and minor triads are of a purely ideological nature. The opponents agree in the ideological starting point of the debate: What they do not notice about harmony is that it is the work of aesthetically interested subjects and their materialism eager for sound enjoyment; but instead they assume the effective force of a higher principle given in nature, according to which the whole world is *constructed* in the truest sense of the word. The most popular arguments are therefore confessions to the respectively own world view, as can be seen from the following polemic against dualism:

"Everything earthly is looking for a support point ... However, if the nature only builds upwards and lets grow, but never also 'symmetrically-contrarily' downward, then the 'will of nature', presented for proof, is non-existent, and the proof is untenable."[2]

---

[1] An example for this stereotypical thinking: *"Major and minor triads have therefore sprung up from one root ... This system is called 'monism' ... Riemann's major and minor triads spring up from different roots ... This is the system of dualism."* (Hermann Grabner, *Allgemeine Musiklehre*, Kassel 1974, p. 155)

[2] Josef Achtélik, *Der Naturklang als Wurzel aller Harmonien*, pt. 2, Leipzig 1922, p. 104.

2. Tonality

a) Cadence

Major and minor triads, the completed shapes of the consonance, enter for their part into harmonic relations: As triads that stand in fifth ratios to each other, they form the elements of tonality. This kind of harmony initially manifests itself in a succession of consonant triads that is called cadence.[1]

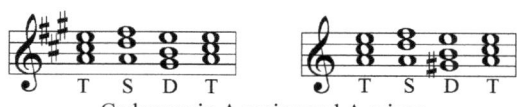

Cadences in A major and A minor

Jean-Philippe Rameau has coined the terms tonic, dominant, and subdominant for the sounds that stand in such a constellation. In the above example, the tonic (T) has the root tone A, the dominant (D) has – a fifth higher – the root tone E, and the subdominant (S) has – a fifth below the tonic root tone – the root tone D. The essence of the cadence, however, does not lie in the relation of their root tones, but in the harmony between the complete triads.

Taken by itself, these triads are merely the – basic or compound – consonances analysed in the first chapter: They have their foundation in the immediate harmonising of the tones, but exactly therefore, they are determined abstractly, that is, independently of the form of the triads and the octave position of the tones. The consonance form as such is exactly *not* what characterises the tonic, dominant, and subdominant, since these are defined by their interrelation, in a similar way as the tones of a triad are defined by their interrelation.[2]

If one considers only the relation of the root tones of the dominant and subdominant to the root tone of the tonic, one again has to do with a consonance here. It is the same consonance that also in the major and minor triads themselves provides the strongest contribution to the harmony of the triads. The fact that these root tones do not sound simultaneously, but one after another, does not change anything in terms of their harmony, whose essence, as already stated, does not lie in the mere vibration ratio of 3:2, but in the accordance of the sound parts of different tones. But, as said before, it is not about the mere relation between the root tones, but about a harmony between complete major and minor triads.

---

[1] *"The cadence is the most perfect expression of tonality."* (Hermann Grabner, *Allgemeine Musiklehre*, Kassel 1974, p. 109)

[2] *"Each chord is what it is – tonic, dominant, or subdominant – in relation to the others. And the result of this reciprocal relationship is the cadence, the model of tonal harmony."* (Carl Dahlhaus, *Studies on the Origin of Harmonic Tonality*, trans. Robert O. Gjerdingen, Princeton 1990, p. 38)

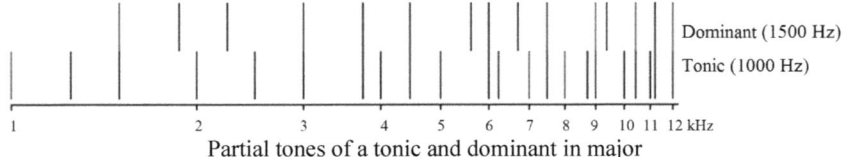

Partial tones of a tonic and dominant in major

In the above example, in which the sound spectra of two successive major triads are compared, 10 out of 15 partial oscillations of the dominant coincide with those of the tonic. In this respect, one is tempted – and the author himself succumbed to this temptation in the beginning – to characterise tonality as a consonant relation of consonances.[1] But one must actually rather speak of a *quasi-consonant* relation here; because, on the one hand, the harmony between the triads is comparable to that between the tones, insofar as it equally consists in the matching of the sounds; on the other hand, it is about other objects that harmonise here; and that gives the harmony a new character. Philosophically speaking, this consonant relationship has thus secretly moulted into a new form of harmony: From a relation between *tones*, it has become a relation between *triads*, and this is precisely the essence of the *tonal* relationship. Consonance, therefore, characterises only the *internal* relation of the major and minor triads; their *external* relation deserves a new name. Consonance is the harmony between *tones*, tonality is the harmony between *consonant triads*.

Every consonant triad can have this harmonic relation in two directions: upwards and downwards. Whenever a triad occurs in this double relation, it is a tonic. The two-sidedly configured harmony of the tonic necessitates, at its opposite poles, a one-sided relation of the dominant and subdominant to the tonic, to their common harmonic centre. The 'counter sounds' (the dominant and subdominant) have furthermore a special relation to each other, which results from their relation to the tonic and which now cannot even be called quasi-consonant any longer:

$$9:4 = (3:2)^2$$

This relation, spanning over two fifths, expresses a harmony that is mediated by the tonic. In the relation of the dominant and subdominant, the tonic is thus *indirectly* included.

The fact that the sound with which the cadence begins is a *tonic* reveals itself to the listener *in retrospect*; because the relations in which the tonic shows itself as such cannot have occurred with the first sound yet. Not until the dominant and

---

[1] In the German edition on which this translation is based, the author still writes: *"The tonality is, if you like, a consonant relation between consonances"*. Although this *"if you like"* is intended to indicate that a certain amount of caution is advised here, the author has ignored this and considered the wording to be an appropriate description. In this respect, the presentation of the tonality had an inaccuracy, which has been corrected in the new version of the above paragraph for the English edition.

subdominant have sounded, do the tonal relations, and thus the tonic and dominants, exist for the perception. *Afterwards*, the tonic immediately appears during its sounding as what it is harmonically. After the confrontation of the dominants, it appears for the perception as a fulfilment of the harmony indirectly contained therein, as a harmonic *resolution* of the tension that lies in the relation of the dominants. In other words: The essence of the resolution into the tonic lies in the termination[1] of the harmonic tension between the counter sounds by exactly the one sound by whose mediation this tension only exists in the first place.[2]

The movement in which the dominants confront each other and resolve into the tonic takes place in two forms:

Authentic and plagal cadence

In the case of the *plagal* cadence, the subdominant fifth turns into the tonic root tone during the process of resolution. This metamorphosis is not effected by this root tone itself, but by the simultaneous appearance of the tonic third and fifth. In comparison, during the *authentic* resolution, the tonic root tone appears as the tone by which the tonic contrasts with the dominant. The tension before the appearance of the tonic is therefore stronger in the case of the authentic cadence, and its effect as a resolution is more intense and more popular so that the terms 'perfect' and 'imperfect' cadence are equally common in the English-speaking world.

The two forms of the cadence are forms in which the tonality realises itself. This tonality is nothing other than the harmonic relation that exists between triads and that finds expression in the definition of these sounds as tonic, dominant and subdominant. An entirely different conception of tonality has gained propagation by Hugo Riemann's *"doctrine of the tonal functions of harmony"*.[3] Riemann defines tonality, in reference to Fétis, who has coined this term, as

"the relation of a melody, of a harmony sequence, even, of an entire piece of music to a main sound as the centre, by the position to which all other harmonies receive their special sense, their meaning for the harmonic logic, for the cadence formation, etc."[4]

---

[1] Hegel would say: "die Aufhebung", i.e. the sublation, in which the aspect of a preservation is also included.

[2] *"In tonal harmony, the dominant and subdominant form a contrast that requires a mediating tonic to restore a balance."* (Dahlhaus, *Studies on the Origin of Harmonic Tonality*, p. 74). It is *"a 'dialectical' contrast between subdominant and dominant that resolves itself in the tonic."* (Ibid., p. 111)

[3] Hugo Riemann, *Handbuch der Harmonielehre*, Leipzig 1918, p. 214.

[4] Ibid., p. 214.

At first Riemann transforms in his theory the *harmonic* relations between consonant triads into relations that have something to do with *sense and meaning*. It is, namely, his intention,

"to present the laws, according to which our mind understands the meaning of the tones in the melody sequence, as well as in the sounding-together with other ones." [1]

In regard to music listening and enjoyment, he confuses – as many others – the capacities of the *perception* with those of the *intellect*. *Aesthetic* relations seem to him therefore to be *logical* ones, in so far as they supposedly allow an understanding. He comes to logical connections in the following way: He ignores the harmonic character in the relations between the dominants and the tonic, and instead assumes that they have a relation of representation characteristic of meanings. According to that, all sounds, except for the tonic, are not they themselves, but in the proper sense *representatives* of the tonic. As such they are supposedly understood *subjectively*, but this – strictly idealistically – with *objective* harmonic consequences:

"Only the chord imagined in its relation to other ones, that is, understood in its logical context, is a consonance or dissonance." [2]

Riemann is far from distinguishing consonance and tonality as forms of harmonising, that is, of the going well together of components. The difference between consonance and dissonance is a matter of comprehensibility for him; it is supposedly the difference of *"understandable on its own"* and *"understandable in relation to the tonic"*. His entire theory of harmonic functions offers a programmatic method to interpret each harmony *"in the sense of"* a sound that is *not* this harmony itself:

"When a harmony receives its full aesthetic value only by its relation to a tonic, ... so is indeed each sound that is not itself a tonic actually not heard as [this sound] *itself after all, but rather in the sense of that sound which is the tonic, that is: Actually, only the tonic chord itself is an absolute consonance."* [3]

Or elsewhere:

"Characteristic for the tonic is its complete consonance, its ability to conclude; since all other harmonies are understood in its sense, none of those, but only it alone is actually satisfying in its own right (absolutely consonant)." [4]

The construction according to which the essence of the tonic lies, as it were, therein that it means itself has no idea that the tonic, dominant, and subdominant are equally qualities that consonances only obtain *as a result* of their relation to each other. Riemann's theory, conversely, presents the tonic as an *autonomously given precondition*, to which the remaining world of sound then only has to refer.

---

[1] Riemann, *Handbuch der Harmonielehre*, p. 1.

[2] Ibid., p. 139.

[3] Ibid., p. 140.

[4] Hugo Riemann, *Allgemeine Musiklehre*, Berlin 1918, pp. 76 f.

b) Dissonance

The cadence is the form in which the tonic, dominant, and subdominant define themselves reciprocally by their harmonic correlation, by following one after the other. In this form, the tonal triads sound as those consonances that form the starting point of this relation. But the harmonic relations between these tonal basic sounds can also occur as a sound combination in which the components of different tonal triads sound together. Such a sound combination is then, however, not a consonance.

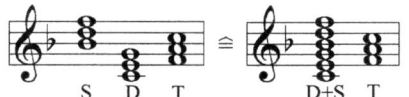

Comparison between a cadence and dissonance

In the above two sound sequences, the subdominant and dominant are juxtaposed to one another and resolved into the tonic. The harmonic substance is the same. Only the form is different. On the right side, the confrontation of the dominants appears in a sound combination and therefore as a dissonance. The resolution of the confrontation of the dominant and subdominant therefore takes on the shape of a resolution of a dissonance.

Thus, the dissonance differs from the consonance in that it contains a tonal relation in itself. It is not a harmony of directly harmonising tones, but of tones that harmonise as components of different tonal triads. It is thereby not always necessary that all elements of a triad occur in a dissonance. The dissonance can combine any tones of the tonic, dominant, and subdominant, so that there is a whole series of dissonances, which can be categorised according to their composition.

In order to simplify the harmonic analysis of the dissonances, the root tone, third, and fifth shall be noted in the following as lines behind the abbreviations of the tonic, subdominant, and dominant. The lines symbolise the positions of the tones in the basic form of the triad: In this harmonic formula, the root tone is noted at the bottom, the fifth at the top. Examples in F major:

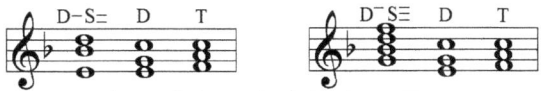

Dissonances consisting of a dominant and subdominant

As far as the emphasis of a dissonance lies on the subdominant, the resolution into the tonic is also commonly mediated via the dominant in order to achieve an authentic movement:

Authentic resolutions of subdominant dissonances

A second type of dissonance is composed of the tonic, dominant, and sub-dominant. Within such a dissonance, of course, the tonic does not have the character of a resolution. As a resolution, the tonic appears only where it sounds on its own, that is, in the form of a consonance.

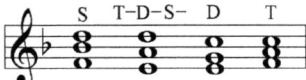

Dissonance consisting of a tonic, dominant, and subdominant

The above dissonance consisting of the thirds of the tonal triads contains the tonic not only indirectly within the relation between the dominants, but very directly. This addition of the tonic, however, has nothing that defuses the dissonance, but expresses the need for resolution into the alone sounding tonic only more blatantly. The resolution itself receives thereby a double determination: It is, firstly, the resolution of the confrontation of the dominants and, secondly, the tonic's dissolving out from the combination with the dominants.

A dissonance consisting of the tonic, dominant, and subdominant must always include the tonic third. Because the root tone and fifth of the tonic are also tones of the dominant or subdominant, and they are also exclusively perceived as such if the tonic third is missing. There is then no reason to assume a dissonance consisting of three tonal basic sounds.

The mildest form of a dissonance is the combination of the tonic with only one of its dominants.

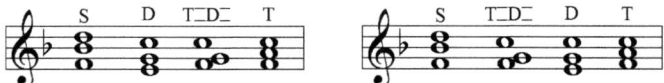

Dissonance consisting of a tonic and dominant in different harmony sequences

This form of the dissonance does not contain the confrontation of both dominants, but only the sound combination of a quasi-consonant relation between consonances, that is, the ratio 3:2 between the tonic and dominant. Consequently, the tonic is a resolution in two respects: On the one hand, it resolves the harmonic tension between the dominant and subdominant, which sound as consonances here, and in whose confrontation the dissonance T⁻D⁻ is only embedded. On the other hand, the tonic is dissolved out from its combination with the dominant, in which it is merely a component of the dissonance T⁻D⁻, thus sounds free for itself as a consonance, and in this limited meaning it is the resolution of a dissonance. The resolution of the *contrast of the dominants* and the resolution of a *dissonance* are two processes here that must be kept apart analytically, but that coalesce in a single incident – the occurrence of the tonic.

Here are further examples of this third type of dissonance:

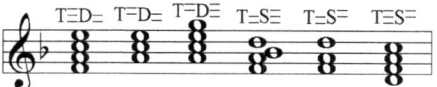

Dissonances consisting of a tonic and dominant or subdominant

The character of a dissonance depends on its composition of tonic, dominant, and subdominant components. However, the fact that the tonic has one tone in common with the dominant or subdominant does not imply in every case that the respective tone is equally a representative of two tonal triads. The mere tonic is and remains a consonance and contains, just because of the common tones with the dominants, nowhere near any dominant tone. If a tone shows a tonic as well as a dominant character in a harmony, then this is an *effect* of the dissonance, but never its *cause*.

The ear hears a consonance if no other tones are added that indicate a dissonance. It hears a *mild* dissonance if it has no reason to hear a *strong* dissonance. It, for example, never hears a dissonance with the formula D^-S^-, but instead the milder dissonance T^-D^-, which consists of the same tones that the first formula assumes. And in order to make a harmony consisting of all three tonal basic sounds accessible to the perception, the presence of the tonic third is indispensable. The musical perception may be harmonically *inspired*, but it is not *speculative*: It adheres to what is offered harmonically.

The harmonic formula of the dissonance illustrates the respective character of such a sound: its composition of tonic, dominant, and subdominant components. It shows the *substance* of the dissonance and thereby its *essence* as a *tonal sound form*. The situation is different with the formulas that do not fixate the *harmonic character* of the dissonance, but its *appearance* as a frequency ratio. More about this in the following.

Every dissonance contains relations between tones that belong to different tonal triads. In the form of the dissonant dyad, such a tone ratio even has an independent form. The associated frequency ratio can each be calculated as a mathematical product of several frequency ratios of the underlying consonances. The frequency ratio between the dominant and subdominant root tone, for example, which can also be found in the dominant seventh chord (D^-S_-), is the relation of two fifths:

$$(3:2) \cdot (3:2) = 9:4$$

The resulting frequency ratio 9:4 (from D to S downwards), the ratio of the so-called ninth, is *only quantitatively* distinguishable from other frequency ratios. *Qualitatively*, it is of the same kind as the frequency ratios 6:5, 4:3, etc. Because in the form of the frequency ratio, not only the specific harmonic character of a dissonance disappears, but also quite generally the basic difference between consonance and dissonance. If one merely looks at the outward appearance of a harmonic relation, then the specifically harmonious at it can easily be overlooked. However, the dissonances can, by all means, also differ in the extent to which the traces of their inner nature get lost in their outward relations. In order to make this clear, the following table illustrates dissonant dyads of a major key with their harmonic formula, the calculation of the corresponding frequency ratios on the basis of their composition out of consonant frequency ratios, as well as the common names for the associated intervals:

no.	formula	consonances	ratio	quotient	name
1	D_S_	(3:2) · (3:2)	9:4	2.2500	ninth
2	D-S-	(3:2) · (3:2)	9:4	2.2500	ninth
3	D¯S¯	(3:2) · (3:2)	9:4	2.2500	ninth
4	T_D¯	(3:2) · (3:2)	9:4	2.2500	ninth
5	T¯S_	(3:2) · (3:2)	9:4	2.2500	ninth
6	T¯S_	(3:2) · (3:2) · (1:2)	9:8	1.1250	major second
7	T¯S_	(2:3) · (2:3) · (2:1)^2	16:9	1.7777	minor seventh
8	T_D-	(3:2) · (5:4)	15:8	1.8750	major seventh
9	T_D-	(2:3) · (4:5) · (2:1)	16:15	1.0667	minor second
10	T-D¯	(3:2) · (6:5)	9:5	1.8000	minor seventh
11	T-D¯	(2:3) · (5:6)	10:9	1.1111	major second
12	D_S_	(3:2) · (3:2) · (5:4) · (1:2)	45:32	1.4063	dimin. fifth
13	D¯S-	(3:2) · (3:2) · (6:5) · (1:2)	27:20	1.3500	fourth
14	D¯S-	(2:3) · (2:3) · (5:6) · (2:1)^2	40:27	1.4814	fifth
15	D¯S_	(3:2) · (3:2) · (3:2) · (1:2)	27:16	1.6875	major sixth
16	D¯S_	(2:3) · (2:3) · (2:3) · (2:1)^2	32:27	1.1852	minor third
17	T-D-	(6:5) · (5:4)	3:2	1.5000	pure fifth
18	T-S-	(6:5) · (5:4)	3:2	1.5000	pure fifth

The table shall help clarify the difference between the essence and the appearance of the dissonance; the structure of this table shall briefly be explained by using the first example: The *formula* D_S_ designates a relation between a dominant (D) and subdominant (S) root tone, where each root tone is marked by a line at the bottom.[1] Between these two root tones lies the root tone of the tonic, whose relation to each of the other root tones is that of a fifth, that is 3:2. In the column *consonances*, the two fifths (3:2) are shown as the underlying consonances, as the factors from which the *ratio* 9:4 (next column) is calculated. In the column *quotient*, this relation is presented as a decimal fraction. In this form, the intervals between the dissonant tones, which also underlie the *names* of the tone relations, can be compared according to their size; however, the concept of the intervals will be thematised only in the sixth chapter – as deduced forms of harmonic relations.

---

[1] The order in which the harmonic components are listed is actually arbitrary; only for the sake of clarity, this book uses a uniform notation: D, T, S.

The table shows and compares dissonances that
  – differ harmonically and are identical by name (examples 1 to 5)
  – are identical harmonically and differ by name (examples 5 to 7)
  – differ in the quotient and have the same name (examples 7, 10)
  – bear the name of consonances (examples 13, 14)
  – sound like consonances (examples 17, 18).

This shall now be examined closer: In a frequency ratio like that of a ninth (9:4), quite *different* dissonances can be presented, as the examples 1 to 5 show. Already the mathematical expression in which this ratio is calculated and which still reflects the ratios of the enclosed consonances contains no longer a reference to the tonal origin of the ratio. Accordingly, a single dyad with this frequency ratio does not reveal whether its components are root tones, thirds or fifths and whether they are of tonic or dominant nature. Only in the context of the sound sequences in which the aesthetics of the tonality unfolds does this dyad present its specific harmonic characteristic.

The frequency ratio 9:4 is, conversely, not the only form in which a dissonance like T‾S‿ appears (examples 5 to 7). On the basis of the harmonic identity of the tones that originates from the harmony of the octave, the same dissonance can assume the shape of a major second (9:8) or the shape of its inversion as a minor seventh (16:9), etc. The variety of the manifestations of a dissonance increases the quantity of the numerical ratios, which, in their external appearance, indicate nothing of their origin. This applies all the more at the surface of the musical aesthetics, in the area of the scales, scale degrees, and intervals, where the harmonic relations go through even further metamorphoses on the basis of the associated frequency ratios. From this sphere not only originate the above mentioned designations for tone relations, but all imaginings of the contemporary music theories as well. What source of confusion the melodic configuration of the harmonic structures can be will become apparent in the sixth chapter.

The identification of dissonances by their frequency ratios is further complicated by the fact that in several cases different ratios are barely distinguishable by the ear. Relevant to the acoustic distinction are the values in the column *quotient*. The quotients of the proportions 16:9 and 9:5 (examples 7 and 10) are so close together that the tone relations are not even distinguished by their name.

$$\text{Minor seventh:} \quad 16:9 = 1.777$$
$$\text{Minor seventh:} \quad \;\;9:5 = 1.800$$

The "difference" between the relations 16:9 and 9:5 is called syntonic comma, whose frequency ratio can be calculated as follows:

$$\text{Syntonic comma:} \quad (9:5):(16:9) = 81:80$$

The syntonic comma is no longer perceived as a tone ratio, but as a nuance in the tuning of a tone. On that basis, even an experienced and very concentrated listener can find out the difference between the 16:9 and 9:5 ratios only in direct comparison. But what is even more serious in this regard is the circumstance that the harmonic character of a sound depends on the tonal "context" in which it sounds, and not at all on how exactly its theoretically determinable frequency ratios are intonated. Conversely, the musical listener can, due to the actual harmonic characteristic of a sound as fixed in the harmonic formula and as determining the harmonic perception, intuitively sense, whether the presented tones are intonated cleanly or not. Just by the sound, the minor seventh does not reveal whether it is made up of two fifths or of a fifth and a minor third, let alone from which harmonic constellation it originates which is composed of such consonances. At best, one can hear that the minor seventh is *at all* a dissonance – but even this only in the very abstract and negative sense that it cannot be a consonance.

But even this abstract form to appear as a dissonance is not characteristic of all dissonances. Because, even the minor third (32:27 in example 16) formed of three fifths is separated from the consonant third (6:5) only by the syntonic comma and can therefore, taken alone, appear as a consonance.

$$32:27 = (6:5) : (81:80) \approx 6:5$$

Hence, the dissonant minor third belongs to the *pseudo-consonances*. Finally, this type of dissonance also includes tone relations that even the most precise measuring instrument cannot differentiate from a consonance: The fifth (3:2), contained in the dissonances T–D– and T–S– in examples 17 and 18 and made up of the consonant thirds of different tonal triads, has, on the face of it, absolutely the same frequency ratio that also characterises the consonant relation between a root tone and fifth in a major or minor triad.

The frequency ratios in which the harmonic relations present themselves are by no means that which establishes the properties of the harmonies. Already the sheer form of the quantitative relation makes any qualitative difference disappear. The relation 16:5 contains greater numbers than the relation 9:5 or 6:5, but what does that say about the definition of a sound as a consonance or dissonance? And even the attempt to extrapolate from the mere frequency ratios to the harmony expressed therein can only succeed exceptionally because of the various possibilities of confusion. Harmonies prove to be what they are according to their concept only in the succession of sounds in which the opposition of the dominants and the resolution into the tonic take place. Harmonies are, in substance, components of this tonal movement.

c) Theories About Consonance and Dissonance

The existing or not existing need for resolution of a harmony gave music theorists the cause to make a qualitative distinction between dissonance and consonance. In explaining this difference, however, they always imagined the harmonies as oscillation ratios, that is, in the very outward form in which the inner relation and the actual harmonic difference disappears in mere numerical ratios. The prejudice of all such theories is that the *qualities* of consonance and dissonance must be searched for in *quantitative* relations. All these theories are looking for a natural boundary between consonances and dissonances, that is, for a *limit* up to which harmonies remain consonances and from which on they become dissonances.

The oldest solution to this puzzle lies in the identifying of quantity and quality. This is the realm of number mysticism,[1] where also Zarlino bustled. One can now also see how the already mentioned explanation of the consonance from the number six came about: This number was expected to have the natural property of not yet being too large for the consonance. Later theorists have tried to combine the quality of the harmonic with the quantity on detours, that is, to find out the ominous boundary between consonance and dissonance by a closer examination of the sound relations. A couple of examples may clarify the logic of this approach: the theories of Helmholtz, Stumpf and Husmann.

Helmholtz transforms first of all the contrast that he wants to explain into one of euphony and cacophony, thus denying from the beginning the beauty of the dissonance. Next he transforms the aesthetic contrast into a physiological one and turns towards the effect of the sounds on the auditory nerve – but in a speculative manner:[2] He claims that beats – a physical effect caused by the periodic superposition of oscillations – are unpleasant to the ear from a certain frequency on.[3] The beats, however, whose frequencies can be calculated from the frequency ratios of the tones, which are thus a derived physical quantity, refer him back to the problem of demarcation that his congenial predecessors had already constructed in reference to the sound relations themselves.

"One circumstance may, perhaps, cause the musician to pause in accepting this assertion. We have found that from the most perfect consonance to the most decided dissonance there is a continuous series of degrees, of combinations of sound, which continually increase in roughness, so that there cannot be any sharp line drawn between consonance and dissonance, and the distinction would therefore seem to be merely arbitrary. Musicians, on the contrary, have been in the habit of drawing a sharp line between consonances and dissonances, allowing of no intermediate links, and Hauptmann advances this as a principal reason

---

[1] *"Also from other fields in which the numbers are likewise effective as qualities ... it could be adduced several things that confirm the exceptional position of the quality seven, as well as the cleft that separates it from preceding numbers ..."* (Ernst Bindel, *Die Zahlengrundlagen der Musik im Wandel der Zeiten*, pt. 2, Stuttgart 1951, pp. 110 f.)

[2] Helmholtz deems the fact that he searches for the cause of the contrast between consonance and dissonance outside the music to be a proof of quality of his theory: *"Hence I do not hesitate to assert that the preceding investigations, founded upon a more exact analysis of the sensations of tone, and upon purely scientific, as distinct from aesthetic principles, exhibit the true and sufficient cause of consonance and dissonance in music."* (Hermann von Helmholtz, *On the Sensations of Tone as a Physiological Basis for the Theory of Music*, trans. and notes A. J. Ellis, London and New York 1895, p. 227)

[3] *"The nerves of hearing feel these rapid beats as* rough *and unpleasant ... The cause of the unpleasantness of dissonance we attribute to this roughness and entanglement."* (Ibid., p. 226)

against any attempt at deducing the theory of consonance from the relations of rational numbers." [1]

With the idea of missing intermediate links between consonances and dissonances, Helmholtz tries to reconcile the problem of the qualitative distinction with the idea of a continuous series. To that end, he again turns towards the music in order to discover tone ratios that *do not* exist:

"The scales of modern music cannot possibly accept tones determined by the number 7 ... Here, then, there is a real gap in the series of chords arranged according to the degree of their harmonious effect, and this gap serves to determine the boundary between consonance and dissonance." [2]

For such a derivation of a difference from a gap, however, the whole construction with the supposedly so "rough" beats would not have been necessary!

A second variant of that kind of theory construction is the tone psychology by Stumpf. He, for a change, does not deny the aesthetic character of the dissonance, but the perceptibility of the tones of a consonance: He claims that, when two tones sound together, more or less the impression arises that one hears only one tone and that the difference of the tones gets blurred for the perception, namely more in the case of the consonance, less in the case of the dissonance. In order to prove this, he makes preferably unmusical test persons guess whether they hear one or two tones.[3] The foreseeable result: The confusion between a unison and a dyad occurs most frequently in the case of the octave. With the frequentness of the acoustical illusions (if not even of the concessions to the desired interpretation of what is heard), Stumpf measures the supposed fusing degree of the tones and demonstrates that there is only a gradual difference between consonance and dissonance if one is willing to interpret these harmonies as more or less fused sound combinations.[4]

---

[1] Helmholtz, *On the Sensations of Tone as a Physiological Basis for the Theory of Music*, p. 227.

[2] Ibid., p. 228.

[3] Also Stumpf is proud of the fact that he looks for the reason of a harmonic difference outside of the music. He reports about the diligence, by which he tries to eliminate the contamination of his study caused by musical judgments, and assesses the suitability of his test persons accordingly: *"Two of the 14 which initially volunteered immediately proved to be ... unusable for the purpose in hand. The one, because he ... not only regularly recognised octaves as two tones, but also called them octaves."* (Carl Stumpf, *Tonpsychologie*, vol. 2, Leipzig 1883, p. 158). But Stumpf also found useful test persons: *"Extreme inability with, by the way, normal hearing acuity and intelligence, I found in the case of Mr. ... Currently, he really cannot repeat a tone according to its pitch. Concerning the question, which of two consecutive tones is the higher one, he gives ... a great many false answers."* (Ibid., pp. 362 f.)

[4] By transforming harmony into a fusion of tones, this turns into a very diffuse and murky affair. The theory explains us the dullness of our senses. This is exactly what comes out when a tone psychologist tackles the manifestations of musicality with quasi-physiological experiments.

36

Husmann finally, who correctly determines the consonance by the coinciding of partial tones, does not, however, distinguish it as a harmonic form from the dissonance, but assumes that there is an *immediate* relationship between the tones in *every* harmony. This is because he also views the harmonies only from their physical side and therefore sees only the quantitative ratios. So he tries to derive the harmonies *as number proportions* from each other, and, in doing so, finds no harmonic difference:

"If one lets the harmonic intervals come out of one another by the harmonic division in this way, then it is hard to understand why consonance and dissonance are supposed to be opposites. It is rather to be expected after all that, to the physical property, since the frequencies of an interval form a very simple relation, also in the area of the soul, only a single peculiarity corresponds, which, according to whether the objective frequency ratio is more or less simple, is also more or less pronounced. By consonance, we therefore want to understand here only the mental property that is the expression of the objectively simple oscillation ratio." [1]

Husmann considers only the vibration ratio to be objective, not the *form* of the harmony. Thereby, the little word 'simple' suggests to be the opposite of 'complicated', for which, however, never factual reasons are presented. So the word 'simple' remains a synonym for relatively small numbers, where, by the way, the quantification *"more or less simple"* is based on. Since the *"soul"* with its ability of harmonic perception and distinction does not *"correspond"* with Husmann's expectations, the concept of the consonance, which stems from the *musical* practice, is simply being defined in the sense of a merely *physical* objectivity.

All the mentioned theories only offer somewhat cumbersome procedures in the attempt to reconcile the qualitative difference between consonance and dissonance with the prejudice that harmonies, in essence, are *number proportions*. The starting point is always the unshakable belief that the difference between consonance and dissonance must be founded *extra-musically*. Then the two harmonic shapes undergo a strange transformation and are what they *are* in a very abstract sense always also a little bit *not*: beautiful sounds, combinations of *distinguishable* tones, *objectively* contrary sound forms, and so on. In this way, different sound forms turn into two extremes of a continuous spectrum. And the end result of such an art of distinction is the *theoretical* resolution of the dissonance into a consonance.

The whole thought movement from the starting point to the end point of the theories about consonance and dissonance can be found briefly summarised in modern lexicon entries. That consonance and dissonance *do* stand in contrast to each other and that they *do not*, is only a few lines apart:

*"**Consonance** ... in tonal music a sound ... with rest and relaxation character in contrast to the dissonance in need of resolution. The tones of consonant sounds stand in simple frequency proportions to each other. However, the conso-*

---

[1] Heinrich Husmann, *Einführung in die Musikwissenschaft*, Heidelberg 1958, p. 124.

nance phenomenon can neither be clearly explained mathematically nor physically. Because the consonance is not a fixed quantity, but a relative sound value concept ... without a clearly determinable boundary to the dissonance ... "[1]

Or expressed even shorter:

"Between consonance and dissonance exists, on the one hand, a gradual difference (the higher consonance level is the lower dissonance level and vice versa), on the other hand, a specific difference or a contrast." [2]

Hugo Riemann translates the unrelated juxtaposition of a qualitative and quantitative determination of harmonies into the differentiation between a "physical" and "musical-logical"[3] consonance or dissonance. He sometimes realises the tonal composition of certain dissonances, but without recognising the harmonic character of the dissonance in it:

"According to this combination of elements of both dominants, this chord (the so-called dominant seventh chord D^7) has a similar potency for closing towards the circumscribed tonic as the succession of counter fifth-chord and simple fifth-chord (S − D) ... The dominant seventh chord conforms fairly accurately to the sounding-together of the 4th, 5th, 6th, and 7th overtones ... The dissonance of the chord is therefore an extraordinarily mild one ..." [4]

The dominant seventh chord is dissonant in Riemann's view insofar as, on the one hand, it supposedly has "to be understood" as a dominant, but, on the other hand, it contains a tone foreign to the dominant. Whether this foreign tone is essentially determined as a subdominant tone or as an equivalent to the seventh overtone is obviously not decisive in Riemann's argumentation. Both determinations serve equally as evidence of the foreign and disturbing in the idealistic construct of a *"unity of the sound meaning"*:

"All chords which, except the root tone, third, and fifth of the sound in whose sense they are understood contain yet one or more other tones, or also one or more other tones instead of the root tone, third, and fifth of the sound, are called dissonant. Dissonance is therefore quite generally speaking: a disturbance of the unity of the sound meaning by foreign elements." [5]

The principle of Riemann's theory of harmony becomes apparent here, a principle that he applies to all objects of his 'function designations': Dissonance, in his view, is a distorted harmony and as such always something negative: a deviation from a supposedly *intended* harmony.

---

[1] Gerhard Kwiatkowski et al. (eds.), *Meyers kleines Lexikon Musik*, Mannheim et al. 1986, p. 186.

[2] Carl Dahlhaus and Hans Heinrich Eggebrecht (eds.), *Brockhaus Riemann Musiklexikon*, vol. 2, Mainz 1998, p. 321.

[3] Riemann, *Handbuch der Harmonielehre*, p. 88.

[4] Ibid., p. 141.

[5] Ibid., p. 138.

d) Key

Tonality is the harmonic relation of the tonic, dominant, and subdominant. This harmony realises itself in a sound sequence that can have quite different forms. It can occur as a cadence, namely either in an authentic or plagal movement pattern. Or, dissonances of various composition can alternate with consonances. The kind of the harmonies as well as their succession is completely irrelevant for the substantial harmony of the tonality which comes into effect in the respective sonic constellations. All of these forms in which the relation of the tonic and dominants takes effect can, however, be summarized in one basic figure: The tones of the tonic, dominant, and subdominant express, quite independently of how they sound together or follow each other as consonances or dissonances, the tonal interrelationship by the totality of their relations to each other. As such tones, they constitute the *tone ensemble of a key*.[1]

A key has thus seven tones that are determined as root tone, third, and fifth of the tonic, dominant, and subdominant:

$$S_- \qquad S^- \qquad S7/T_- \qquad T^- \qquad T/D_- \qquad D^- \qquad D^-$$

This ensemble of tones – in whatever form it appears – contains the tonality as its law. Accordingly, the perception intuitively decomposes all sound sequences realised from this tone ensemble into the basic sound components so that the resolution into the tonic is perceived as harmonious. The tone ensemble of a key is not just *any* expression of the tonality, but its *decisive* form of existence, which contains everything that constitutes the tonality. It offers with its inner relations the material for the perception of the tonic.

Thus, the keys differ in their tone ensembles. Different tone ensembles also arise depending on whether the tonal components are major or minor triads. This difference has not been dealt with so far, because the concept of the cadence and dissonance is independent of the 'tone gender'[2] of the triads. Now, it has to be clarified to what extent *major and minor* triads underlie the formation of keys.

The characteristic of the cadence and dissonance has been explained using the example of a major key, which consists of three major triads. This also revealed the phenomenon of the pseudo-consonance, to which now one has to come back. In a major key there are three dissonances that are structured just like minor triads:

---

[1] *"By the three triads of the tonic, dominant, and subdominant, the key is completely and exhaustively determined."* (Rudolf Louis and Ludwig Thuille, *Harmonielehre*, Stuttgart 1907, p. 3). This sentence should give thought to every enthusiast who reads a lot of deep meaning into the key.

[2] *"In western music theory, keys, chords, and scales are often described as having* major *or* minor *tonality, sometimes related to* masculine *and* feminine *genders ... German uses the word* Tongeschlecht *("Tone gender") for tonality, and the words* Dur *(from Latin* durus, *'hard') for* major *and* moll *(from Latin* mollis, *'soft') for* minor.*"* (https://enacademic.com/dic.nsf/enwiki/550797, 1 October 2019)

Three pseudo-consonances in F major

The first two dissonances contain the consonances with the frequency ratios 6:5 and 5:4, where, however, each of the consonances innately belong to two different basic triads, in both cases. The third sound contains the ratio 5:4 of the subdominant and the ratio 32:27, that is, the dissonant third, which is composed of the subdominant root tone and dominant fifth. The above example, thus, contains three sounds that would be considered minor triads outside the presented context, but are dissonances in the tone ensemble of a major key. In addition, the seeming consonances stand in a fifth relation (3:2) to each other, hence they behave like the dominant, tonic, and subdominant of a complete pseudo-tonality. If these sounds were not just *seeming* consonances, but *real* ones, then, conversely, the major triads would be dissonances of a minor key. This much, however, has the analysis of the tonality already revealed: The relation of the consonance and dissonance cannot be reversed. The same sounds cannot be consonances and dissonances at the same time. In the tone ensemble of a key, the tonic must be unambiguously determinable, otherwise there can be no such thing as tonality.

As a matter of fact, the tonic is undoubtedly identifiable in every key. Hence, the ear must have an objective harmonic basis for its "decision" regarding the question of a real or seeming tonality. The reason why the sound sequences from the tone ensemble of a major key are resolved into the major tonic is that the major triad is the stronger consonance. The consonance schemata in the first chapter show that more partial frequencies coincide in the major triad than in the minor triad. On this basis, the consonant internal relations of major triads emerge, in a corresponding tone ensemble, as harmonically dominating.

There can therefore be no tonality of three minor triads, however much this has been claimed by nature mythologists with their abstract notions of symmetry. So the question arises by what confrontation of dominants a harmonic resolution into a minor tonic can come about at all. Two *minor* dominants instantaneously turn out to be pseudo-consonances. Two *major* dominants resolve into a major tonic. Hence, it can only be a *combination* of major and minor triads that leads to a tone ensemble which constitutes an alternative to the major key.

Either the dominant or the subdominant must be a major triad. For this purpose, one can do a little experiment: How would a minor tonality sound with a major subdominant?

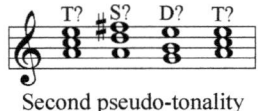

Second pseudo-tonality

In this sound sequence, the ear recognises very quickly the tone ensemble of the key of G major and feels the immanent tonality of this tone ensemble, which is why it prefers the following resolution:

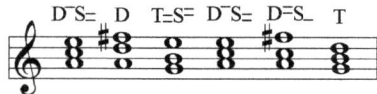

Resolution into the tonic of G major

Thus, it is the *dominant* that has to be a *major* triad:

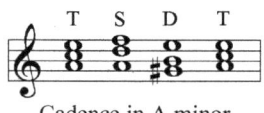

Cadence in A minor

There is only *one* possible alternative to the tone ensemble of a major key: a minor key with a major dominant. The opposition of a major dominant and a minor subdominant is an unmistakable harmonic constellation of sounds that reveal themselves as antipodes of an autonomous tonic. At the same time, the subdominant, as a minor sound, lays a harmonic foundation with which a minor tonic fits well because on that basis all of its tones stand in consonant relations to the according tones of the subdominant.

e) Primitive Tonality

The analysis of the tonality took its starting point from the consonance, that is, from the major and minor sounds. Now it becomes apparent, how these basic sound forms occur in the tonal music: What counts as a major or minor sound and therefore as a consonance, cannot be determined independently of the tonality developed from these categories. The tonality separates the consonance from the pseudo-consonance. Hence, it has its own precondition as its result.

This state in which the tonality creates its logical basis itself can only have emerged from a primitive tonality which was not yet based on the distinction between consonance and pseudo-consonance, but which had this distinction as a result. This transition took place during the Renaissance.

The basis of the beginning Renaissance music were the church modes (also called Gregorian modes). These are the medieval tone scales formed from a common tone ensemble, each spanning an octave, and differing only in the way in which the tones are *treated*: different tones can each

– form the starting point of a scale,
– play the role of the final tone (finalis) in vocal music,
– act as a sustained tone (tenor, repercussa, reciting tone).

The church modes fixate the modalities of the psalmody, that is, the medieval main form of solemn speech song, of the ritual monotony. The term psalmody is nowadays generally used quite rightly as a synonym for cult recitation,[1] and the adequate term *modal music* designates – rightly as well – a music based on a recitation tone. This kind of music, which was and still is in use in all pre-bourgeois societies, is, by the way, totally independent of the particular interval structure of the tone scales, which is completely irrelevant for the above-mentioned universal principle of modal music. Number and tuning of the tones were based on a harmonic speculation, with which, on the one hand, it was recognised that the music *has* a harmonic basis; on the other hand, this harmonic basis was not developed *as such* because the religious rite remained the really decisive foundation.

In so far as the ensemble of the seven medieval tones was formed from consecutive fifth steps (3:2), the resulting tones had, on the face of it, a certain similarity with the tone ensemble of a major key. During the nascent polyphony, exactly these tones were taken as a basis when trying out sound sequences which, from the perspective of the developed tonality, largely sound like a staying in pseudo-tonality.

Hans Judenkunig, Christ ist erstanden (final bars), Vienna 1523 [2]

Archaic tonality

In this example, consonances have been strung together in a way that already reveal initial approaches of a resolution into a tonic. At any rate, the music was supposed to end with a consonance. From the perspective of the developed tonality, this would be guaranteed if, instead of the G (encircled), a G sharp were written. In that case, a major dominant would provoke a resolution into an A minor tonic, what obviously comes closest to the idea of the composer, but, on the other hand, does not fit into the frame of the church modes.

In the *isolated* perception of the harmonies, the deficiency of this archaic tonality does not stand out. But the livelier such music is played, the more the harmony that is included in such a sound *sequence* asserts itself, that is, the tonality of a major key, for which a resolution into a major sound seems to be appro-

---

[1] Cf. Eberhard Thiel, *Sachwörterbuch der Musik*, Stuttgart 1984, p. 527.

[2] Sheet music from an editing by Siegfried Behrend (*Altdeutsche Lautenmusik für die Gitarre*, Hamburg 1959, p. 5., © courtesy of Musikverlag Hans Sikorski, Hamburg). What Behrend has already transcribed into the notation of the tonal music for the musical performance *practice*, is complemented in the above example by a harmonic annotation which also *theoretically* applies the standards of the tonal music and therefore extrapolates the corresponding tonic from the tone ensemble of the key of C major.

priate. Conversely, the attempt to resolve sound sequences into a minor sound leads to an instinctive adjustment of the used tone ensemble. Thus, the primitive tonality itself contains the germ to the development of the major and minor keys, in whose ensembles of tones a finished tonality with a defined tonic manifests itself.

Helmholtz and other music theorists assume that from very early on the G sharp in A minor was occasionally sung divergently from the notated G, which, however, was strictly forbidden to the entire Christianity already in the 14th century:

"It was blamed in an edict of Pope John XXII., in 1322, and in consequence the sharpening of the leading note was omitted in writing, but was supplied by the singers, a practice which Winterfeld believes to have been followed by Protestant musical composers even down to the sixteenth and seventeenth centuries, because it had once come into use." [1]

This edict demanded that the singing had to obey religious and not aesthetic criteria:

"In 1324/25 Pope John XXII. decreed in the Constitutio docta Sanctorum *the preservation of the modesta gravitatis of the singing against the lascivia of the novellae scholae discipuli, whose compositions were banned from the Church under threat of punishment."* [2]

Even in the transition period of the tonal music, musicians still had to be very careful so that their "vulgar" deviations from the prescribed mode would pass unnoticed. This shows the following incident: Henricus Glarean interpreted in 1547 certain innovations that he observed in music as new modes, which he introduced under the names of "Ionian" and "Aeolian". However, these precursors of major and minor scales were in no case tolerated.

"But in the Middle Ages the Aeolian mode was considered illegitimate. So to be able to fit the melody into the octoechos, *one had to categorize it either as Hypophrygian or as Hypodorian ... That is, to conceal the chromatic f♯ one notated the melody with the* finalis a *instead of* e. *(Only in the antiphonary of Lucca is the melody handed down with the* finalis e, *and there the f♯ is omitted.) ... On the other hand, it is hardly a superficial matter that the notation of the Petrucci print of 1503, which may be taken as authentic, maintains the appearance of the mode being Hypolydian."* [3]

The modal music is incompatible with unbiased music enjoyment. Its cultivation is a matter of creed, namely in social systems in which there is no escape from religion. Accordingly, the purpose to which the cultivation of music is

---

[1] Helmholtz, *On the Sensations of Tone as a Physiological Basis for the Theory of Music*, p. 287.

[2] Carl Dahlhaus and Hans Heinrich Eggebrecht (eds.), *Brockhaus Riemann Musiklexikon*, vol. 1, Mainz 1998, p. 57.

[3] Carl Dahlhaus, *Studies on the Origin of Harmonic Tonality*, trans. Robert O. Gjerdingen, Princeton 1990, p. 265 and pp. 269 f.

subjected is defended against every temptation to be interested in the music for its own sake. The sinful human is prone to deviate from the monotony of the psalmody. Before, however, the tonal music can arise out of it, not only the societal conditions need to be changed, but also the principles of a complete aesthetics must be developed, which utterly results from the essence of the music. That this could not happen overnight will be clear in the further analysis of this aesthetics. But once the tonal music is complete and familiar to everyone, it can very quickly displace the modal music in its today's refuges. In an Islamic theocracy, this does not require much more than, for example, the lifting of an import ban on Western musical instruments.

3. Aesthetics of the Modulation

a) Key Relationships

The keys, in whose ensembles of tones the tonality crystallises, are the starting point of a *third* type of harmonic relations. The first chapter dealt with the harmonising of the *tones*, which is perfected in the *consonance* of the basic sound forms, that is, the major and minor triads. The second chapter was about the harmonic relations into which these *basic sounds* for their part step to each other, that is, about the *tonality* effective in the tone ensembles of the keys. In this way, the basic shapes of the tonal music are successively built: as aesthetic forms of which each one for its part becomes the starting point of *relations of fitting-together*, that is, of relations in which sound components of the same kind go well together in each case. The next subject in this systematics is the harmonic relation in which *tonal tone ensembles* come into a relation to one another. Such relations realise itself in the transition from one key to another key, that is, in the *modulation*.

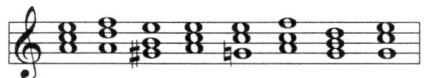

Modulation from A minor to C major

One can see here how at first the tone ensemble of the key of A minor with its inherent tonality constitutes itself. The key of C major then opposes it with its own tone ensemble and causes by its own tonal relations that a resolution into the tonic of C major is expected.

The ensembles of tones are what the keys are summarised in, wherein they have their harmonic consistence, and wherein they differ from each other. Hence, also the harmonic relation between the keys lies in the accordance which their different tone ensembles present. On this basis, keys go well together.

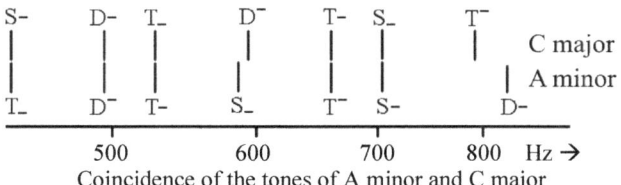

Coincidence of the tones of A minor and C major

Both of the keys, A minor and C major, have six tones in common: A, B, C, D, E, F. These tones belong to different tonal basic sounds and to keys with different root tones and tone genders, but as tones, they coincide. This is precisely where the harmony lies in the transition from one key to another. In reference to Husmann's 'coincidence theory of consonance', it can be said that the harmony included in the transition between keys is only correctly explained by a 'coincidence theory of modulation'.

The commonality of the tone ensembles does not depend on whether the tone relations are exactly the same in both keys. The dissonance 32:27, made up of three fifths, and the consonance 6:5 differ, as has already been shown, only by the syntonic comma (81:80), which is no more perceived as a relation of different tones. Consequently, the commonality in the tone ensembles of two keys is not affected if a tone of the one key is higher by a syntonic comma. In the following example, it does not matter that the tone D has either 587 or 594 Hz:

Three of the common tones of A minor and C major

Musicians when playing particularly precisely can come very close to the pure tone ratios so that they intonate the tone D in C major accordingly higher than in A minor if their instruments (for example stringed instruments) allow this. However, this is not necessary and, in the case of the tempered tuning, it is not a problem at all, when before and after a corresponding modulation the tone D is played in a uniform and constant tuning.

As little as the tuning of a tone disturbs the harmony between the keys, so much does it conversely all come down to how noticeable the distance of the tones is in which tone ensembles differ from each other. The keys of A minor and C major are distinguished by the tones G sharp and G. The ratio between these tones is the same as that between the thirds of major and minor triads with the same root tone:

$$(5:4) : (6:5) = \mathbf{25:24}$$

This ratio is called *small* semitone, namely in contrast to the *major* semitone, which, in major and minor keys, lies equally between the dominant third and the tonic root tone:

$$D–T_- \;=>\; (2:3) \cdot (4:5) \cdot (2:1) = \mathbf{16:15}$$

Between the small semitone and the syntonic comma lies, according to the order of interval sizes, the comma that is called 'enharmonic diesis' (128:125), which, for example, occurs in the relation between the keys of A minor and F minor, namely between A flat and G sharp (encircled in the following illustration):

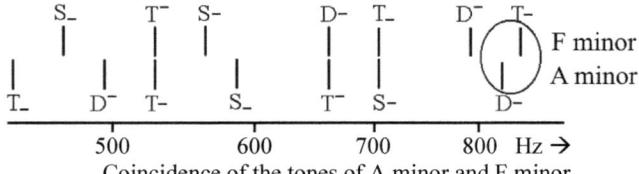

Coincidence of the tones of A minor and F minor

The keys of A minor and F minor do not have three, but four common tones because even the comma 128:125 does not constitute a relation between two different tones. The harmony between the keys of A minor and F minor appears even more clearly in the tempered tuning:

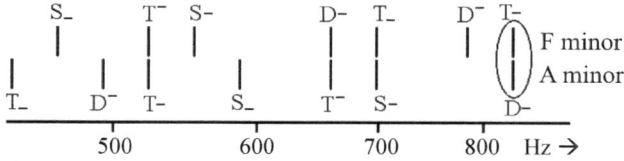

Harmony between A minor and F minor in the tempered tuning

The small semitone is the smallest relation between tones that are kept apart in the musical practice and perception. Whether tones, in the comparison of the keys, are the same or not is thus dependent on whether their relation lies in the range of a comma or already in the range of a semitone, that is, whether by their frequency ratio an obviously existing threshold is exceeded or not in the perception of tone relations.[1]

One can now see that, in the harmonic relation of the tone ensembles, the tone has to be determined independently of its tuning. The immanent harmonious character of the tone relations, their determination by the consonance and tonality, is not impaired by minor deviations from the harmonically pure frequency ratios. Hence, the further representation can well dispense with these pure tone relations the way they were quoted so far for a better understanding because it is abstracted from them in the modulation.

The tone, thus, proves to be an *abstract* tone not only by the consonance of the octave, but furthermore by its determination in the relation of the keys as well. The abstraction from the changing tunings which a tone can take on within the frame of the modulation is the basis of the equally tempered tuning, in which the tuning of each tone is kept constant. In the case of the equal temperament, there is not even a distinction between the small and major semitone, but instead the octave is evenly divided into twelve semitones.[2] It is not a coincidence that this tempered tuning prevailed when baroque music, on a solid tonal foundation, brought the principle of modulation to full blossoming. Because the twelve tones of the tempered tuning form a tonal system in which there is no limit on the transition from one key to another: No key can have a harmonic relation to another key that is not likewise presentable in this tonal system. Consequently, any transition into another key can be intoned within this tonal system with its twelve fixed tones.

---

[1] The fact that the *musical* perception has a greater tolerance than physical measuring instruments when identifying tones reveals itself in the *music*, and not in the examination of the aural sense. *Acoustic* and *physiological* experiments in order to prove the perception threshold that is decisive for the *musical* differentiation of tones are therefore not only superfluous, but also totally out of place.

[2] The difference between the small and major semitone is 128:125.

In the following, the tempered tuning is taken as a basis because it is also helpful to simplify the presentation of the harmonious relations of the keys. This makes it easier to see that each key can, in principle, harmonise with 23 other keys because the twelve tones are the sufficient basic material from which a total of twelve major and twelve minor keys can be formed, each with their unique tone ensembles.[1] And since every tone ensemble has seven tones – that is more than half of the twelve fixed tones –, two keys involved in a modulation must always have at least two common tones.

	C	C#	D	D#	E	F	F#	G	G#	A	A#	B
C major	•		•		•	•		•		•		•
C# major	•	•		•		•	•		•		•	
D major		•	•		•		•	•		•		•
D# major	•		•	•		•		•	•		•	
E major		•		•	•		•		•	•		•
F major	•		•		•	•		•		•	•	
F# major		•		•		•	•		•		•	•
G major	•		•		•		•	•		•		•
G# major	•	•		•		•		•	•		•	
A major		•	•		•		•		•	•		•
A# major	•		•	•		•		•		•	•	
B major		•		•	•		•		•		•	•
C minor	•		•	•		•		•	•		•	
C# minor		•		•	•		•		•	•		•
D minor	•		•		•	•		•		•	•	
D# minor		•		•		•	•		•		•	•
E minor	•		•		•		•	•		•		•
F minor	•	•		•		•		•	•		•	
F# minor		•	•		•		•		•	•		•
G minor	•		•	•		•		•		•	•	
G# minor		•		•	•		•		•		•	•
A minor	•		•		•	•		•		•		•
A# minor	•	•		•		•	•		•		•	
B minor		•	•		•		•	•		•		•

The tone ensembles of the 24 keys

Based on the above table, it is easy to see that there are different degrees of correspondence between the keys. Keys that have relatively many common tones harmonise particularly well. One can also say that there is a close *relationship* between these keys,[2] and this is only right as another expression for this har-

---

[1] Referred to the piano keyboard, *"every key requires the use of a unique combination of black and white keys."* (Gerhard Marhold, Tastatur von Tasten-Musikinstrumenten mit durch Farbe, Form oder sonstige Merkmale unterschiedenen Tasten eines Manuals, in: *Das Musikinstrument*, no. 5/1986, p. 78)

[2] *"The fewer common tones two scales have, the more distant is their kinship."* (Christoph Hempel, *Neue Allgemeine Musiklehre*, Mainz 2001, p. 130). In German, one speaks of a kinship (Verwandtschaft) of the keys, in analogy to the biological kinship.

mony. The fact that this relationship is, all too often, explained wrong and is not even recognised as a form of harmony is another matter.

From the table of the tone ensembles, the degrees of relationship between the keys can be identified. If the starting key is the key of C major, the next related keys are the keys of G major, F major and A minor. This is followed by D major, B flat major, C minor, D minor and E minor. The reason for this, however, is not the fifth or third in the relation of the root tones as is the unanimous opinion of textbooks, but the degree of coincidence of the respective tone ensembles.[1] If we consider only the major keys, then this fallacy still has a certain semblance of plausibility. Because the harmony between the major keys seems to decrease the more the root tones of the keys move away from each other in consecutive fifths. In the case of the (harmonic) minor keys, such a deduction of the relationships between the keys from root tone relations is much less plausible.

If choosing the starting key a semitone higher, then the next related keys also appear chromatically raised. The harmonic relations between keys can be transposed and can therefore be presented in a form that is valid for all starting keys. The following overview shows how many tones a certain major key has in common with each of the other 23 keys.

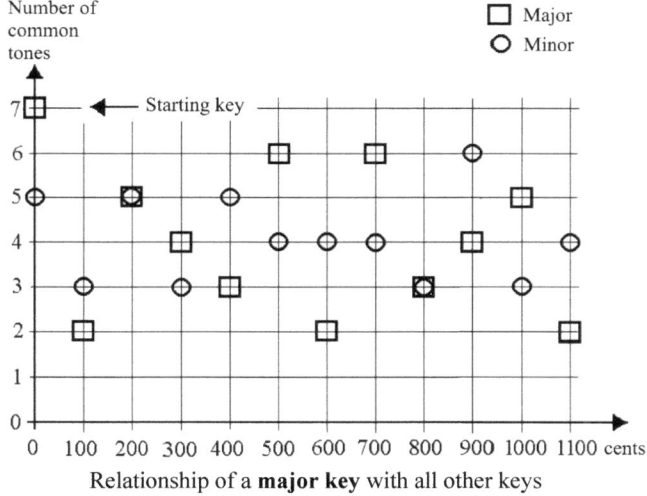

Relationship of a **major key** with all other keys

Another diagram results if the starting key is a minor key:

_____

[1] An example for the incorrect deduction of the relationship between the keys: *"Directly fifth related are the keys that are next to each other in the circle of fifths: C major and G major ...* Indirectly *fifth related are the keys that have an* intermediary *fifth related key in common, that is C major and D major (through mediation by G major) ..."* (Hermann Grabner, *Allgemeine Musiklehre*, Kassel 1974, p. 71)

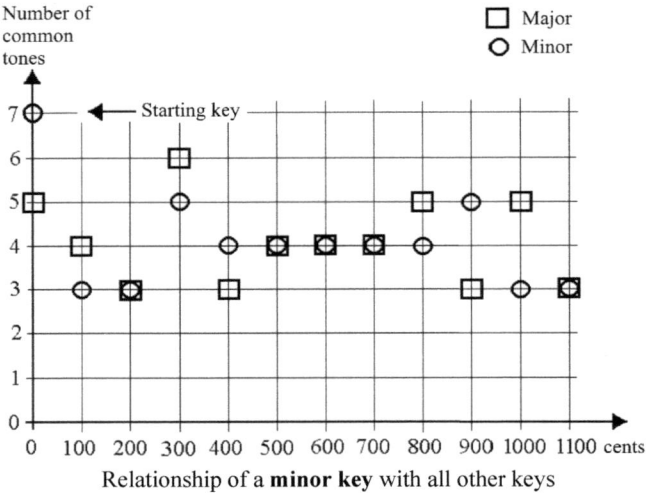

Relationship of a **minor key** with all other keys

The keys are represented here by their (tonic) root tones (the key tones), whose relations to each other are indicated in cents. This unit is a logarithmic measure for frequency ratios based on the tempered tuning. 100 cents correspond to one tempered semitone; 1200 cents correspond to an octave.

The relationships between the keys are usually clarified by the circle of fifths, which, however, is not suitable *for this purpose*. Everything that can be visualised with the circle of fifths is the logic of the key *signature*:

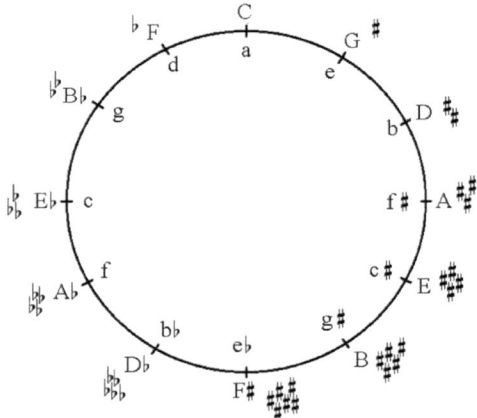

The circle of fifths

The notation of keys is a completely *practical* matter, which is furthermore based on *melodic* relations, which will be analysed in the sixth chapter. This practice has nothing to do with the explanation of *harmonic* relations. The current music theories, with their idea of fifth and third relationships, turn even the third main form of harmony into the material of their confusion of harmony and frequency ratio. They do not take into account that the modulation is based exactly on the abstraction from the precise frequency ratios. The difference in the harmonising of the tones, triads, and keys is overlooked as a matter of course.[1] Accordingly, no music theory has yet addressed the forms in which the sound figures fit together, as well as their respective place in the structure of the musical aesthetics.

b) Process of the Modulation

The harmonic relation between the keys is realised in the modulation, in the transition of one key to the other. In order for such a transition to occur, a starting key has first to constitute itself.

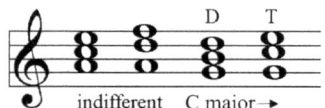

Constitution of the key of C major

In this sound sequence, the key of C major appears with the *third* sound. Both of the sounds *before* can still belong to different keys. While they are being perceived, the feeling for a tonic, which is expected as a harmonic resolution, does not yet arise. *Before* the occurrence of the third sound, the identity of a key has to become apparent yet. *From there* can, in the progression of the harmonies, the key of C major constitute itself, but the key of A minor as well:

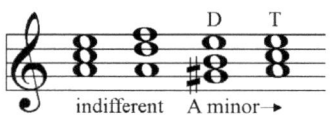

Constitution of the key of A minor

During the constitution phase of a key, the harmonic perception *searches*, so to speak, for the tonality. But it *finds* it only if the presented sounds exclude any uncertainty. That is the case, at the latest, when the tone ensemble of a key has fully emerged, that is, in the above-mentioned examples each time when the third sound occurs. As soon as such a sound appears as a representative of a key, its tonal character, which can be indicated by its harmonic formula, asserts itself as well.

---

[1] For example: *"Fifth related are keys and sounds, whose root tones stand in the relation of the pure fifth."* (Grabner, *Allgemeine Musiklehre*, p. 70)

However, the constitution of a key does not necessarily presuppose that all the tones of a key sound. The ear can also identify a key in fragments of the tonal opposition and resolution if a confusion with other keys is excluded in the presented tone relations.

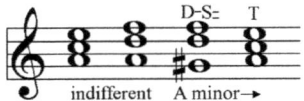

Constitution of the key of A minor

Also in this sound sequence, the key of A minor constitutes itself with the *third* sound. For this purpose, only six tones from the tone ensemble of the key of A minor had to appear; because this combination of tones can only occur exclusively in A minor. With the third sound, any indifference is eliminated, and the key of A minor appears by unmistakeable tonal relations.

Only *after* the constitution of a key can a modulation occur. The second requirement of a modulation lies in the appearance of a sound that does *not* belong to the tone ensemble of the key into which the ear has settled in.

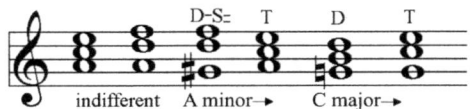

Modulation from A minor to C major

The fifth sound in the above example cannot belong to the tone ensemble of the key of A minor. This sound, thus, disables, nullifies, and invalidates the key of A minor together with its tonal relations. On this basis, the harmonic perception strives to settle into a new key. But in order to do so, no new constitution phase needs now to be passed through. Because the essence of the modulation does not lie in the fact that keys constituted independently of each other are combined externally. Modulation is a harmonic transition in which the harmony between the keys, that is, the partial congruence of their tone ensembles, realises itself.

Hence, the harmonic perception not only assumes that the sound which invalidates a key belongs for its part to a key, but also that this key harmonises optimally with the nullified key. In principle, that is, detached from the harmonic 'context', the fifth sound in the above example can belong to the keys of C major, C minor, G major, and so on. But as much as the key of A minor has faded away, it is nevertheless the key to which the new key puts itself in a relation. It is the tone ensemble of *this* key that the tone ensemble of the new key compares itself with. From the standpoint of the optimal harmony, the fifth sound proves to be a representative of the key of C major because this key is more closely related to A minor than any other key in which this sound could occur.

Thus, the fifth sound not only *invalidates* A minor. At the same time, it *puts* C major *into effect* and immediately determines itself as a dominant in this key. In this dual characteristic, it is a modulating sound. The immediate presence of the key of C major is thus based on the harmonic comparison of the tone ensembles. The new key does not have to build up like an initial key. That is why the following tonic immediately works as a harmonic resolution. It appears as a resolution not because of the *real* opposition of the dominants, but because of the, in relation to the previous key, instantly enabled tonality, in which, *in substance*, this opposition is included.

If the sound modulating to C major is followed by a sound that *cannot* belong to C major, then this is a further modulation.

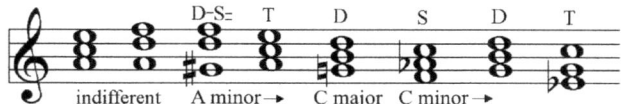

Modulation from A minor to C major and from C major to C minor

Also the *sixth* sound in the above example has a modulating character: It puts into effect one of the keys in which its tones can occur, namely, exactly the key that is most closely related to the key of C major. It is this C minor. The *fifth* sound could *also* belong to the tone ensemble of C minor, but it can, *during* its sounding, only modulate from A minor to C major. The ear assumes, namely, the maximum accordance between the tone ensembles. At *this* point, there is no reason to presume a more distant relationship. Even the subjective knowledge of the further harmonic progression does not cause an *objective* transition to C minor at this point. At most, the hearer anticipates in his imagination the subsequent modulation from C major to C minor.

A *direct* transition from A minor to C minor could look like the following:

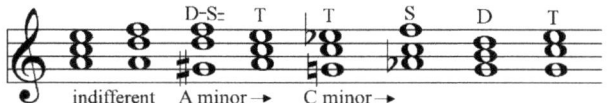

Modulation from A minor to C minor

The modulating sound can only be a representative of C minor here because all other tone ensembles in which its tones are contained stand in a more distant relationship with A minor.

It can also occur that a sound which is incompatible with the previous key can belong to several tone ensembles which all have the same degree of relationship with the invalidated key. In the following example, the sixth sound can appear in both B flat major and C minor. Both keys, however, coincide equally in five tones with C major.

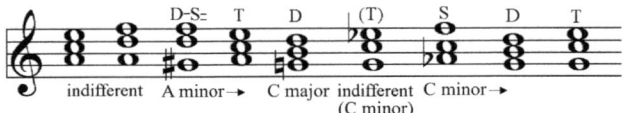

Resolution of an indifference into the key of C minor

In the case of the sixth sound in this sound sequence, the ear cannot decide and waits for the harmonic progress. By further, subsequent tones, it can then be determined at the seventh sound which key comes into question and which not. *During* its sounding, the sixth sound is ambiguous; *in hindsight* – therefore noted in brackets –, it can be perceived as part of a key's tone ensemble. In the above case, a transition to C minor arises, in the following case, a transition to B flat major.

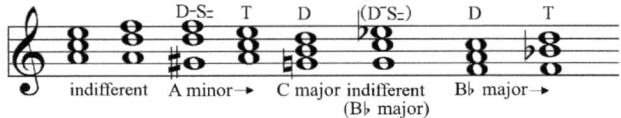

Resolution of the same indifference into the key of B flat major

In the case of a temporary harmonic indifference, the transition is not effected by a *single* modulating sound, but by a modulating sound *sequence* with a specific role distribution: The first sound *nullifies* a key without *implementing* a new key, the second one puts a key into effect while the previous key is already invalidated.

There is still another possibility to resolve a tonal indifference: The indifferent sound is followed by a harmony which does not belong to any of the keys in question, but yet brings a harmonic certainty to the sound sequence.

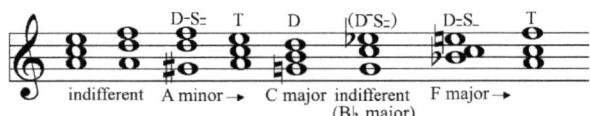

Indirect resolution of a tonal indifference

Here, the ear is offered a modulation from B flat major to F major in the seventh sound. The appeal of this offer lies in the particularly close relationship between the keys of B flat major and F major, which have six tones in common. For this purpose, however, the perception must be able to retrospectively take the indifferent sound as a sound in B flat major and to drop the possibility of C minor. In this case, the ear evaluates the harmony of two successive sounds in their overall effect. The sound modulating to F major produces in doing so, at the same time, the starting point of this modulation: It provides its precursor with a tonal identity on the basis of which it can present itself as a representative of a closely related key. *In one and the same act*, it thus puts into effect the preceding key and, at the same time, the key whose representative it is. In this case, the harmonic intuition waits to apply, on every offered occasion, the criterion of *maximum accordance* between the keys, which has been internalised by attention and exercise.

If a tonal indifference is *not* resolved by subsequent sounds, but instead completed by a further indifference, then a retroactive integration of the tones into a sequence of modulations is no longer possible. Conversely, a tonal indifference can be prolonged in order to pull the harmonic ground from under the listener's feet and, after dizzying harmonic escapades, to lead him back into tonal realms. An example:

Tonal indifference in a gigue by Bach[1]

The first sound of the cited passage stands, on the basis of the preceding sounds, in F major. The next sound modulates to B flat major, followed by a diminished seventh chord (D=S=) that can only belong to the key of C minor, which coincides in five tones with B flat major. The fourth sound – also a diminished seventh chord – could *equally* belong to the keys of F minor and A flat minor. Both keys have four tones in common with C minor so that neither of the two keys can clearly qualify by a closer relationship with C minor. Hence, the sound remains harmonically indeterminate and is not tonalised by the subsequent sounds. Because these are all, regarding their outer shape, diminished seventh chords, which, in chromatically descending order, lengthen the indifference. Although these sounds have the *structure* of dominant-subdominant dissonances (D=S=), they do not have their harmonic *character*; for they do not prove themselves to be combinations of dominant and subdominant tones because they do not create tonality in their succession.

The impression that the cited passage evokes in the music listener is not at all based on a capitulation of the perception to a possibly too complicated harmonic sequence, but – quite the contrary – on the actual characteristics of what the perception finds: The tonal indifference remains, in fact, definitely unresolved across several sounds. These are sounds that do not belong to any key and for which no tonic exists. One can call these sounds *potential dissonances*; because each of these sounds could turn into a real dissonance of a particular key by a suitable subsequent sound.

In the case of such excursions into the tonal no-man's-land, any connection to a previous key that could form a starting point of a modulation breaks off. The

---

[1] J. S. Bach, Partita 1, BWV 825, bar 32 to 40 of the gigue (simplified notation).

re-entry of ensured tonal relations occurs therefore not as a transition from one key to another, but as a renewed constitution of a key.

Quite similar is the situation with a sounding-together of tones that does not occur in any key. Also in this case, the connection to the previous key gets lost, which is therefore not available as a starting point for a modulation. Such *atonal* sounds as for example the so called Tristan chord (F, B, D sharp, G sharp) are not *dissonances* that can be resolved into a tonic, but *disharmonies*, whose "resolution" can only happen in the form of the re-entry of tonal relations, in which a new key constitutes itself.[1] Disharmonies are sometimes used to underline a tragic or comic mood, for example as coquetry with musical inability.

c) Tonal Analysis

With the analysis of the three basic forms of the harmonising, all terms and concepts that are required in order to clarify the harmonic procedure in a piece of music have been developed. For a succession of harmonies, it can be indicated in which key the particular harmonies stand and which tonal basic sounds – that is: tonic, dominant or subdominant – they are composed of.

Such harmonic findings can, in principle, also be achieved intuitively: The music listener can, with an appropriate harmonic attention, develop a sense for the process of the confronting of the dominants and its dissolving into the tonic. He then notices this process even in the case of changing keys and is usually able to recognise a tonal resolution as such. Also a key change can, with appropriate practice, be recognised intuitively.

However, one can also deceive oneself about the quality of what one hears. The analysis of the tonality has already shown that there are dissonances which sound like consonances when listening directly and separately and therefore expose their real harmonic character only in the frame of a sound sequence. The series of harmonic deceptions that can confuse the empirical observer can be completed on the basis of the concept of the modulation as the following example shows:

---

[1] The Tristan chord has, without fault of its own, entered into an excited debate as to whether it should be understood as a harbinger of a principle departure from tonality. It is namely very important for modern composers and their craving for recognition that, on the one hand, the own compositions are highly original and different from all previous creations, but also, on the other hand, that they are very much in line with the trend and therefore legitimised by exactly these previous creations. The composer Schönberg was therefore not only in search of a replacement for the tonality, but also of evidences of an unstoppable erosion of this harmonic *law*, which he considered only as a *convention*. The Tristan chord, seen as a novelty in a development towards something ever newer, was then exploited to prove the inevitability of a historical necessity that Schönberg has executed with his inedible compositions.

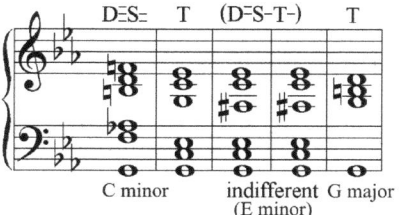

J. S. Bach, Prelude, BWV 999 (ending)

Pseudo resolution to G major

Here, at first, a dominant ninth chord (D≡S≂) in C minor is resolved into its tonic. Hereafter, a tonally indifferent harmony appears, which could equally belong to the keys of G minor and E minor. The last sound presents itself as a G major tonic, which resolves the indifference by retroactively making a modulation from E minor to G major appear as the sound sequence with the greatest harmony.

The impression that this sound sequence creates for the ear is, on the one hand, determined by the fact that the last dissonance remains unresolved. It is the starting point for a modulation to G major. The modulating sound, on the other hand, is a tonic and therefore not in need for resolution itself. What this sound really resolves is not the preceding dissonance, but its tonal indeterminacy. A tonal resolution of this dissonance could at most be effected by a tonic in G minor or E minor. *This* resolution, however, has become unnecessary because of a modulation. Since, however, the dissonance, which during its sounding is in need for resolution, is "settled and done" by a tonic, the illusion arises as though the modulating tonic has resolved the previous dissonance. Such a pseudo resolution even causes an elegant and impressive ending as the above example shows. However, if one takes the harmonic illusion theoretically at face value, then one treats the last dissonance regardless of the therein contained tones as a G major-dissonance, and such ignorance towards the determinacy of a key by its tone ensemble is common practice in the popular methods of harmonic analysis.[1]

The terms developed here explain why and when certain harmonies in a harmonic sequence are perceived as a resolution. They can therefore also be taken as a foundation for a harmonic analysis that makes itself independent of harmonic deceptions. Such a harmonic analysis has to proceed, based on the already described characteristics of the modulation, in the following way: It has to

- determine which starting key constitutes itself,
- determine whether the key is maintained or invalidated,
- find the compatible tone ensembles of the modulating sounds,

---

[1] Most of the note examples that were cited in discussions in order to refute the theory presented here were, as a matter of fact, pseudo resolutions that nonetheless were taken for "true" resolutions.

- find the tone ensemble with the maximum accordance to the previous key,
- take into account the subsequent sound in the case of a tonal indifference,
- determine the basic sounds (tonic and dominants) of the found key,
- determine the harmonic composition of the sounds.

This method of the harmonic analysis can be formulated as an algorithm, which can be converted into a computer program. The harmonic findings to the following prelude by Johann S. Bach come from such a computer program.[1]

J. S. Bach, The Well-Tempered Clavier I, Prelude I, BWV 846 (simplified)

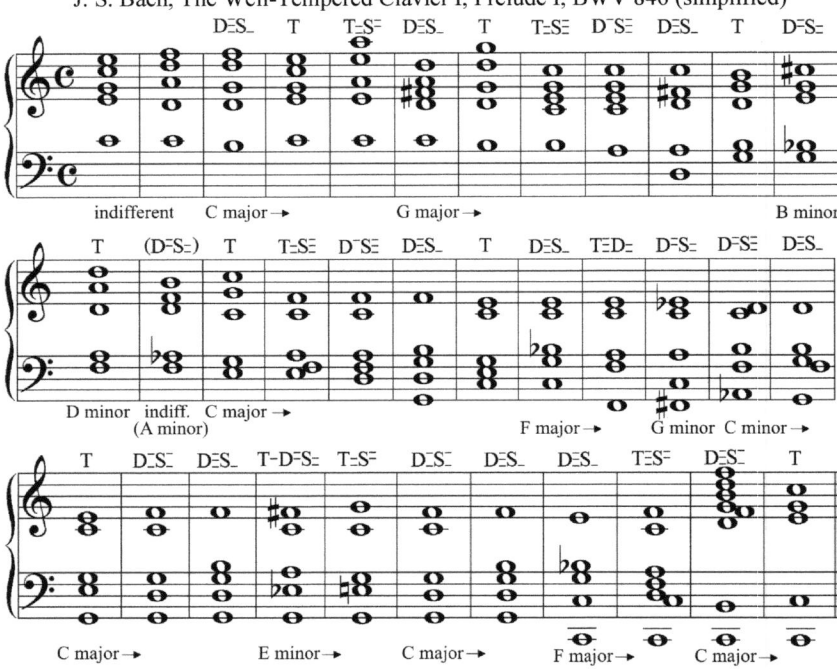

Harmonic structure of a piece of music

<hr>

[1] Together with Jörg Teschner, the author constructed a "tonal sensor" in 1987, which analyses the keyboard playing of a synthesizer in the manner described here and simultaneously displays the harmonic findings on a screen. The device was intended to be used to control the tone tuning of the music played depending on the found tonal key according to the just intonation. Although the project has been abandoned because of some problems that have to do with the determinations developed in the next chapter, the concept of the "tonal sensor" has, nevertheless, been reason to the here elaborated analysis of the modulation process. The core ideas of this theory of the modulation were first presented at the beginning of 1988 during the presentation of the developed instrument at the Hochschule für Musik und darstellende Kunst in Hamburg. A print of the lecture can be found in: Tonale Analyse und Suche nach reiner Stimmung, *Neue Musikzeitung* 2/1988, Ausgabe Schulmusik, pp. 48 f.

Some harmonies are notated in such a way that obscures the view of the respectively played key. Such spellings are known by the name "enharmonic change":[1]

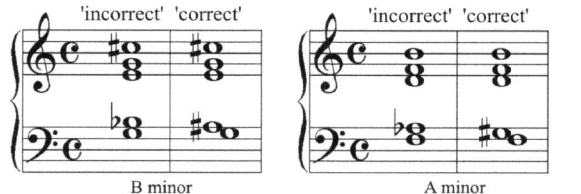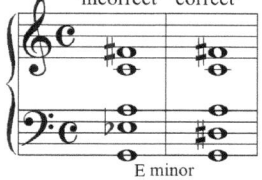

B minor	A minor	E minor

Enharmonic change

The music notation has primarily the pragmatic aim to designate the tones to be played. For this purpose, deviations from a quite existing convention of notating the tones of a key are common and useful. One can anyway not hear how the tones have been notated. With more complicated harmony sequences, the enharmonic change does not even stand out since the key played in the respective case is not so easy to determine. The tonal analysis has to stick to the harmonic facts – the notation does not. But also in other respects, one does not need any music theory in order to make music. In this respect, the correct explanation of the musical laws is a fun in itself that leads to nothing but clarity in the mind.

Clarity, however, is not necessarily what the current theories on the modulation bring to light. These theories consider the relationships between the keys to be completely separate from the process of the modulation. The latter is not understood as the *realisation* of a harmonic relation between the keys, but as a *method* to lead over to a new key. According to Riemann,

"modulation, in the narrower sense, is understood as the obtaining of a new tonic by means of reinterpretation of harmonies from functions of the old key to such of the new one."[2]

The construct of the reinterpretation can only be defined circularly: Where does the new key come from, to which the harmonies are to be reinterpreted and which in fact already contains the tonic, but which at the same time is to be obtained *"by means of reinterpretation"*? The construct of the reinterpretation contains the absurdity that the transition to *another* key is supposed to be effected by exactly such tones in which the respective keys *coincide*. The new key is supposed to already announce itself *before* the transition to the new key is executed. It is not the principle of accordance between consecutive tone

---

[1] *"With the tempered tuning (…) enharmonically distinguished tones coincide in a single one (F sharp = G flat). – 'Enharmonic change' is the merely writing-technical and, for reading purposes, more practical permutation of two such equally sounding tones."* (Gerhard Kwiatkowski et al. (eds.), *Meyers kleines Lexikon Musik*, Mannheim et al. 1986, p. 95)

[2] Hugo Riemann, *Handbuch der Harmonielehre*, Leipzig 1918, p. 216.

ensembles and the therein founded definiteness of the tonal transitions that this theory understands as the inner law of the modulation, but rather a purported goal-directedness of the music towards the new key.

"Mostly, the modulation occurs by reinterpretation. By this, one understands the mediation of the transition by a chord common to both keys, which in a way serves as a pivot point of the modulatory movement by changing its functional meaning that it had in the old key with the new meaning of the target key '(reinterpretation)'." [1]

Grabner, too, masters the circular reasoning: The change to a new key is supposed to ensue *by* a change in meaning that occurs *with* the change to the new key. The reinterpretation is meant to explain the modulation, and the modulation, reversely, the reinterpretation.

Where the theory of the reinterpretation does not find its ominous "common chord" at the key change, it immediately denies any harmonious character and any inner connection in the sequence of harmonies and calls the according transition "abrupt modulation":

*"**Abrupt modulation**: sudden key change, without a mediating transition and without a restriction to degrees of relationship between the keys; is not considered a modulation."* [2]

---

[1] Grabner, *Allgemeine Musiklehre*, p. 131.

[2] Kwiatkowski et al. (eds.), *Meyers kleines Lexikon Musik*, p. 329. In the English translation, this sentence seems even more absurd than in German where "abrupt modulation" is called "Rückung" (approximately: the moving, the displacing, the shifting) and "modulation" is "Modulation".

II. Rhythmics

4. Equability of the Harmonic Succession

a) Transformation of Harmonies into Bars

The harmonic substance of the tonal music unfolds in the succession of the harmonies. The aesthetics of this movement is based on its formal character as a sequence of transitions from one harmony to another. The section between the harmony changes appears in this succession in each case as the sound duration of a harmony, in fact, regardless of whether this harmony really continuous to sound until the beginning of the next harmony. Exactly their sound duration is the criterion according to which the harmonies can compare themselves in their succession. The fourth principle of the tonal music is therefore the accordance of the harmonies in respect to their sound duration or, what is the same, the equable sequence of the harmonies.

The simplest form of this aesthetics consists in a sequence of harmonies with a constant sound duration:

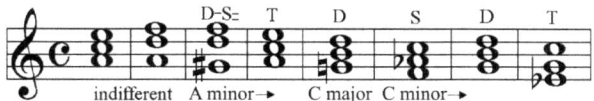

Absolutely equable harmony sequence

This example of a harmony sequence used in the third chapter can serve here as an example of an equable harmony sequence since the harmonies are now written as *bars*. Because this is exactly what the bar lines tell the musician: that the contents that sound between them are of equal duration. The symbolic characterisation of the harmonies serves here only for the clarification of a very abstract statement, which, however, is very crucial: The individual sounds *differ* harmonically from each other so that, at the bar line, a *harmony change* occurs. On this basis, the harmonies follow here one another always in the form of bars.

In this simple form, the bar shows itself very directly as the, to the harmonies adhering, reflex of their equable movement. The bar is, according to its nature, the coinciding sound duration of the harmonies. Expressed as a property of the individual harmony, the bar is the sound duration of this harmony as far as it compares itself with previous harmonies or sets a standard for subsequent harmonies.

The *concept* of the bar which is being developed here must not be confused with the *notation* of the bar. The *notated* bar has, indeed, its basis in objective facts which are the subject here, and mostly reflects exactly the bar *audible* in the music, but, at the same time, it is subject to certain pragmatic conventions, which have by all means their justification. However, the identification of the bar takes place in musical practice not so much with regard to the harmonic movement itself than with regard to its derived manifestations, as will soon become apparent.[1]

The equable sequence of harmonies can also take place in the following form:

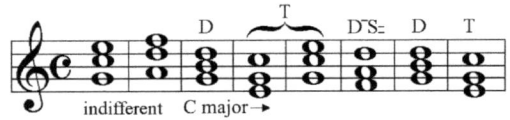

1st form of a maintained harmony

Between the fourth and fifth bar, *no* harmony change takes place. Both bars contain the tonic in C major. In the above example, the tonic appears in two *different* forms (as the first and second inversion of the basic form). There are still two further possible forms: The harmony can be repeated in the *same* form (for example only as the first inversion) so that two bars contain exactly the same tones:

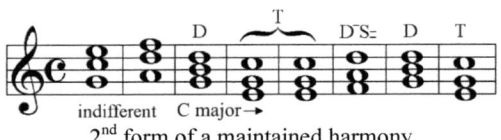

2nd form of a maintained harmony

It is also possible that such a harmony is continued without interruption over the length of two bars:

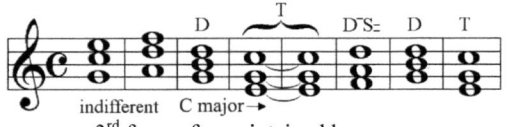

3rd form of a maintained harmony

---

[1] From observations of the following kind, music theorists usually do not draw any conclusion on the concept of the bar: *"The ear, however, is accustomed to understand the step across the bar line as a change of the harmony, not only as a change between weak and strong beats. We place a particular emphasis on this sentence as it is of great importance, not only for the harmonising, but for the analysis as well."* (Johannes Schreyer, *Lehrbuch der Harmonie und der Elementarkomposition*, Leipzig 1924, p. 42). *"First of all, it can generally be stated that the stronger a value is, the more it makes one expect a change of the harmony ..."* (Hugo Riemann, *Grundriß der Kompositionslehre*, pt. 1, Leipzig 1916, p. 51). It does not occur to the authors that these peculiar customs and expectations might be founded in the bar.

All these examples have in common that the harmony change is suspended, or positively: that a harmony is maintained over several bars. The harmonic movement stagnates at such a point so that a harmonic tension or its release is prolonged and thereby intensified.

A typical feature of this form of the bar is the sporadic separation of the bar length and the sound duration of a harmony, whose unity, however, is the permanent basis: The bar constitutes itself by the equable movement of the preceding harmonies, which, with their initially constant sound duration, set the benchmark, to which even the unchanged harmony is subjected. The established bar affects this harmony in such a way that it defines the point in time to which a harmony change is to be expected. If this change does not take place, then the bar turns into a merely passive feature of the prolonged harmony, whose dissection into bars is only effected by the preceding harmony movement. The prolonged harmony itself does not participate actively and in a benchmark-setting way in the constitution of the bar. On the other hand, it cannot escape in this way the immanent determination of the bar to be part of an equable sequence of harmonies.

In the case that the harmonies with a longer sound duration are predominant, it is then *they* that determine the bar so that each quicker change of harmony takes place *inside the bar*.

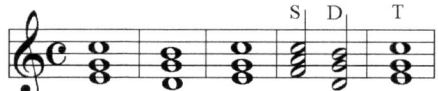

Harmony change inside the bar

Here, too, is the bar the sound duration of the evenly succeeding and therefore benchmark-setting harmonies. The longer harmonies determine the impetus of the movement and establish their sound duration as the length of bars. Sporadically quicker harmony changes consequently take place *within* such a bar and are recognisable by the harmonic contrast of the successive bar phases. The shortened harmonies do not define a bar, but only place themselves with their extravagance in an oppositional relationship to the installed bar, to which they are subjected.

The majority ratios between the harmonies that follow each other quicker or slower can also change so that the change of the prevalent tempo at which the harmonies change appears as a change of the bar.

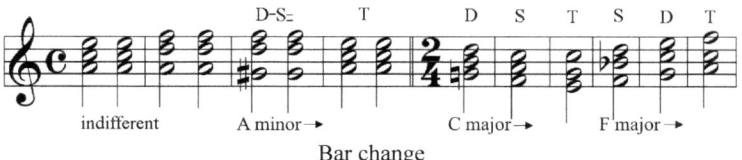

Bar change

The bar change does not, of course, contradict the concept of the bar. The equability of the harmonic movement, which underlies the bar, takes effect before and after the bar change. And even the ratio in which the changing bars stand to each other contains a certain momentum of accordance.

In the case of the examples so far, the bars are notated according to their concept and principle. For the last example, one would, for the sake of a better readability, usually choose a notation that assumes a uniform bar for the whole piece. A bar change is usually notated only if there are good reasons for it. For the musical realisation of the notes, it is namely quite the same whether two real bars are notated as *one* bar or also vice versa. The equability of the harmonic movement comes about regardless of such a notation. Mostly, one prefers the spelling that requires less bar lines.

However, every musician has difficulty to play by notes if the notated bar is in no rational relation to the real bar or if the bar lines are entirely omitted. Because in this respect, too, the musical notation is a tool that takes into account the characteristics of the musical aesthetics. No wonder then that the bar line, as well as the bar itself, is a genuine product of the tonal music.

The freedom given to a certain extent in notating the bars gives the impression that the bar itself is determined entirely independently of the harmonies. The *notated* bar is, as a matter of course, viewed as the *epitome* of the bar because it is virtually the only form in which a bar is taken note of. Conversely, a bar that deviates from the written bar and is merely *heard* does not play a role at all in practice and is not registered by musicians either. In a similar way, many musicians are aware of the key only in the sense of the key signature, that is, as the form in which a whole piece of music is written.

The music theories provide, for these popular views, the seemingly appropriate theoretical construct of a bar that is nothing more than a section in a piece of music, which in turn can, in principle, be dissected into smaller or bigger "units". In treatises on metrics and rhythm, they treat, so to speak as proof of this view, the bar in the context of bar groups, which are formed into phrases in many dances and songs and which, as such, underlie certain close forms (full close, middle close, false close, etc.) – which in turn are often confused with features of the cadence. This aesthetics of phrasing, however, is a specialty of certain musical styles and genres (in the case of Bach, one usually finds them in suites and chorales, but not in preludes and fugues), and hence has nothing to do with the general determinations of the tonal music, which are the subject of this book. These stylistic peculiarities stand thus in no necessary relation to the bar; and the conclusions which are to be drawn from the concept of the bar run in a different direction.

b) Fragmentation of the Bar Content

The harmonies take on the shape of bars by their *equable movement*, that is, in principle, as a result of the fact that they compare themselves to each other after the criterion of their sound duration. Their sound duration functions in this movement as a benchmark that the harmonies set for each other and that therefore is, conversely, also always set for them from the outside in each case. The harmonies are therefore essentially *bar contents*, that is, that which is sounding in the frame and in the course of bars.

The simplest form in which the harmonies spread within the bar is the, until now for the sake of convenience assumed, form of chords in the sense that all tones are sounding simultaneously and during the entire bar:

Anne Bredon/Jimmy Page & Robert Plant, Babe I'm Gonna Leave You (1969)

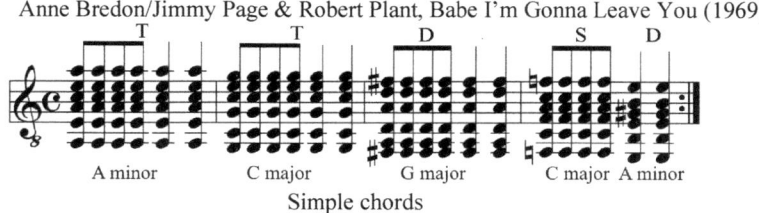

Simple chords

From the determination of the harmony as a bar content, it follows, however, that the components of a harmony do not have to appear at once with the beginning of its sounding and during its whole sound duration. It is sufficient if the respective tones sound at some point in the course of this period of time:

Anne Bredon/Jimmy Page & Robert Plant, Babe I'm Gonna Leave You (1969)

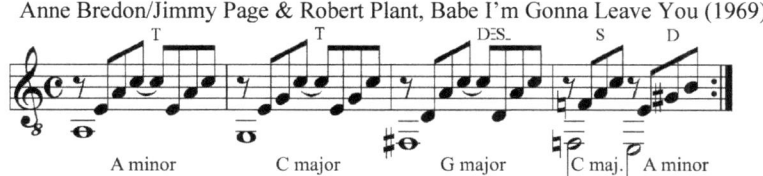

Fragmented harmonies

One can see: The duration of a harmony is the period during which the components of that harmony occur. The sounding-together of the tones is identical with their coexistence in the same bar or bar segment.

Accordingly, every harmony is perceived as a, within the bar, summarised unit of the step by step appearing harmonic particles. The hearer intuitively grasps the points at which the harmony changes take place. The criterion according to which the harmonies are identified results from the definition and character of the bar: It lies in the assumption of a sequence of harmonies that is as even as possible.

When notating a musical idea, a composer might initially be in doubt where to draw the bar lines. He maybe writes the notes without the bar lines at first, then tries out alternatives of drawing the bar lines, and eventually gives preference to one variant. He does not have to know the reason, but it can be named: The optimal notating intuitively considers the logic of the bar and chooses that variant in which the transitions between the harmonies have the following features:

1. They must occur in as *equable* as possible time intervals.
2. They must occur between as *distinguishable* as possible harmonies.
3. They must occur between sounds containing as much as possible *harmony*.

According to the same criteria, also the harmony change inside the bar is recognised. In the case of the above example, a harmony change is sensed in the fourth bar, in fact, both because of the harmonic contrast of the two bar halves and because of their respective consonance:

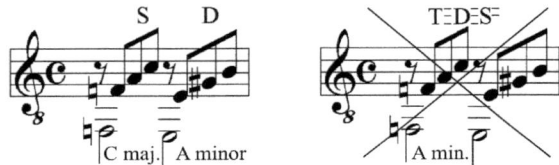

Tonal findings with and without regard to the harmony change inside the bar

Each bar half sounds, taken by itself, more harmonious than the combination of the two halves, taken as a sound unit. Therefore, a transition between these halves is noticed. In the case of the other bars, the bar halves do not differ harmonically at all, so that there are no objective indications for the assumption of two harmonies within one bar.

The bar is the form that the harmonies take on because of their equable movement. In this movement, it constitutes itself and is noticed as a bar, but then also appears retroactively as a property of the first harmony. Thereby, it is even conceded to the first bar that it begins with a pause because its actual length can be derived from the subsequent harmony movement. In the musical notation, the pause is notated at the beginning of a piece of music if it extends over a smaller part of the bar. Otherwise, a shortened first bar is easily recognised on the music sheet even without notated rests and is then called upbeat (pickup, anacrusis).

M. Jagger/K. Richards/A. L. Oldham, As Tears Go By (1966)

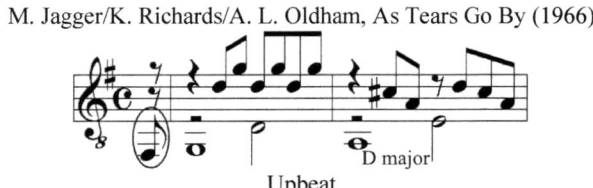

Upbeat

By the way, whoever notates or plays an upbeat does not need to know anything about the harmonic movement which he or she intuitively takes into account. As already indicated, it will yet become apparent that a musician becomes aware of the bar due to its deduced form determinations.

c) Modulating Bar Content

Since the components of a harmony are dispersed inside the bar and sound together as a bar content, the perception of the harmony logically extends to its entire sound duration and is not completed until the end of the harmony. Hence, the specific character of a harmony usually reveals itself only at the end of the bar. In this respect, the perception goes through different phases in the course of the bar in which the sounding tones are step by step registered and harmonically assessed.

For the modulation, this results in a typical form of progression. On the one hand, the new key starts with the modulating harmony, that is, in the moment of the transition into the harmony whose tones belong to a new key. On the other hand, the new key is only clear when the modulating harmony has completely appeared. The harmonic transition has always already taken place when it reveals itself as such. Two examples shall illustrate this:

J. S. Bach, Prelude (BWV 999), bars 37/38

Modulation from G major to C minor

Bar 37 modulates from E minor (in the not shown bar 36) to G major so that G major is the starting key of bar 38, which shall be examined more closely.

1. The first tone, G, still fits into the key of G major. At this point, no modulation is noticeable yet. The same still applies to both the following tones B and D.

2. The tone F is new because it replaces the F sharp which has sounded in bar 36 (not shown) and was still effective in bar 37. At tone F, it is noticeable that the key of G major is no longer in effect. This tone does not belong to the tone ensemble of G major any more. For the tones G, B, D, F that have occurred up to this point, only the keys of C major and C minor come into consideration. According to the, in the last chapter, described principle of the modulation, that is, so to speak, according to the "inertia law of harmonic listening", C minor is ruled out because it has only four tones that also occur in G major, whereas C major has six such tones. The subsequent repetition of the tones B and D confirms the temporary impression that a change into the tone ensemble

of the key of C major is happening. If one stopped playing the piece at this point and was looking for the adequate tonic, then it would become apparent that the ear is attuned to C major.

3. The tone A flat reveals that the harmony with the tones G, B, D, F, A flat cannot belong to the key of C major and that obviously a modulation to C minor is taking place after all. But the starting key of this modulation is not C major, but G major. This is because the modulation does not take place between the components of a harmony, but instead in a sequence of harmonies, that is, in the moment of the harmony change. The key of C minor is therefore the result of the comparison of the tones G, B, D, F, A flat with the preceding key of G major. If the tone A flat were referred to C major, it would appear as G sharp of A minor. In summary: Within a harmony, no modulation takes place, but only corrections of a provisional impression if necessary.

4. Only at the end of the bar, after the repetition of the tones B and F has confirmed the impression of a modulation to C minor, it is definite that this key has become effective. The now completed harmony belongs to the key of C minor. The change into this harmony was therefore a transition from G major to C minor. This transition *took place* at the beginning of the bar, but was *noticeable* only at the end of the bar.

Another example:

J. S. Bach, Prelude (BWV 846), bars 27/28

Modulation from C major to E minor

1. After bar 27, which is in C major, bar 28 begins with a G, which does not yet give any indication of a new key.

2. The tone E flat (in the bass) shows that the key of C major is no longer implemented. The tones G and E flat (respectively D sharp) can belong to different keys of which B flat major and E minor are closest related to C major. Both keys have five tones in common with C major. At this point, thus, arises the impression of a tonal indifference. If the playing is stopped here, it cannot be decided whether the tonic of B flat major or of E minor appears as a better harmonic resolution. The subsequent tones A and C do not contribute anything to the decision in this regard because they equally occur in E minor and B flat major.

3. Only the F sharp makes it clear that the key of B flat major is no longer an option and that, hence, a modulation to E minor is taking place. Therefore, the tone E flat was actually notated "inappropriately" (namely by means of an

enharmonic change) because, in the key of E minor, this tone is usually notated as D sharp.

4. Since no new tones come in addition, it is beyond doubt at the end of the bar that the harmony presented in the bar stands in E minor. A tonal indifference had not really occurred, but it was just not immediately clear which harmony would appear in the course of the bar.

The laws of modulation have not been altered by the bar: The transition of one key to another is a thing that occurs in the moment of the harmony change. That the harmonies come along in the shape of bars, has merely the consequence that the character of a harmony reveals itself not until the end of the bar. In the course of the bar, the components of the harmony appear step by step, giving only a provisional impression of the harmonic progress. If the perception already lets itself be impressed by incomplete harmonies, it has to correct its impressions if necessary. In any case, no modulation takes place within the sound duration of a harmony.

What is now apparent, however, is the more precise nature of the tonal music and the specific ability of the harmonic perception: The determination of the harmonies, the identification of their key and of their tonal composition presupposes, in some circumstances, the identification of the bars. But conversely, the determination of the bars also presupposes the distinguishability of the harmonies. The equability of the harmonic movement *presupposes* the identity of the harmonies and, at the same time, establishes the bar as a *precondition* for determining the harmonies. In order to be able to enjoy harmony and rhythm, the perception equally requires indications for the regular transitions between the harmonies as well as for the transitions between the keys – that is something which cannot always be achieved entirely independently of each other.

Musicality is an ability that easily masters this "problem" when creating and perceiving music. It is less easy to write a computer program that simulates this mental performance, for example by automatically finding the bar lines in an improvised piece of music. The derived shapings of the bar analysed in the next chapter offer, indeed, further reference points for the identification of the bars, but also further aspects for the confirmation of the here already recognisable result that the bar, in a certain way, creates its own basis. The question of the historical "initial spark" for these self-reinforcing tendencies of the bar therefore still remains to be clarified as well.

5. Equability of the Bar Division

a) Segmentation of the Bar

The previous chapter showed the bar as the shape that harmonies take on when they are subjected to the principle of their equable sequence: The bar is the rhythmic sound figure in which the components of the harmony sound together, namely, by appearing in the course of its sound duration. In this context, the relation of the tones is merely of interest in terms of its *harmonic* side, as a relation that they have as components of the harmony summarised within the bar. The following is about the specifically *rhythmic* relation of these tones. Their sounding together in the bar has, namely, its own aesthetics insofar as the appearance of the individual tones takes place on the basis of an equable subdivision of the bar. Hence, the bar is the starting point of a division of its sound duration into time sections which match for the very reason that they are the result of an equable division.

The simplest form of this accordance becomes apparent in the bars that are exclusively dissected into bar halves or thirds. This is the form of the equable sequence of moments in which tones use to appear.

Simple division of the bar into halves

The bar *designation* is, by the way, not identical with the *logic of the bar division*. The notation of the above example as two-four time was certainly also done considering certain ideas regarding the tempo. The quarter note is not defined in relation to the *bar*, but in relation to the *whole note*. In this respect, the idea to define approximate tone lengths, developed in the age of the mensural notation for a still tactless music, has been preserved in a modified form for quite practical reasons. In this sense, the three-four time is not written by the use of "*one-third* notes", but by the use of *quarter* notes. The bar signature, nevertheless, gives an indication of the division of the bar, namely, by defining beforehand the relation of the whole note to the bar. In the above example, the bar signature says that, in its scope, the duration of a bar is described by a half note and that this bar is in principle divided into halves.

The equability of the bar parts resulting from the principle of the division is, however, just the simple starting point of the rhythmics lurking inside the bar. Even at the division of the bar into four equal sections, it becomes apparent that the fundamental accordance of the bar parts is not confined to the equable sequence of the bar quarters. In the quartered bar exists an accordance of the bar halves as well. These halves are not merely included in the division into quarters as a mathematical by-product, but instead are conversely, from an aesthetic standpoint, the higher form of the accordance, which includes the subdivision into quarters. This is because the bar halves not only compare themselves as time periods with each other, but also in respect to their equable subdivision. The division of the bar into four parts is therefore in the first place a halving of the bar and secondly a halving of the bar halves.

Also the quarters of the bar can again be subdivided and so on. The division of the bar first takes place as a division of its entire sound duration and then continues in stages as a division of the bar parts. The segmentation of the bar goes, insofar, beyond the simple form of the bar division and is elaborated as a hierarchy of division levels.

The following example shows a consecutive halving of the bar, bar halves, bar quarters and bar eights. In the notation itself, the structure of the bar division is indicated by the manner of grouping together the sixteenth notes.

J. S. Bach, Prelude (BWV 846)

Hierarchy of the division levels when divided by 16

A bar or bar segment can be divided into *two or three* segments. This is then referred to as an *even or uneven* division. The following example shows a consecutively uneven division of the bar.

J. S. Bach, Prelude (BWV 876)

Hierarchy of the division levels when divided by nine

The dissection of the bar into four, eight, sixteen, or also nine segments always results in an explicit hierarchy of the division levels so that the perception of the lowest division level always also includes simultaneously the perception of the entire hierarchical bar structure that lies above it. The situation is different with the segmentations of the bar in which even and uneven divisions are combined as is the case with the following bars:

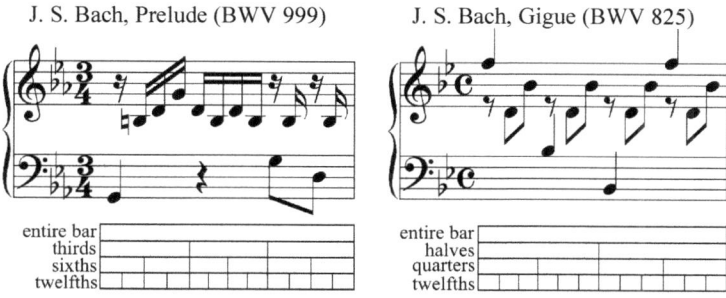

Different forms of the division by twelve

In the first example, the bar division is primarily uneven, in the second, primarily even. In both cases, the segmentation of the bar is *clarified* by the form of the notation, but, of course, it does not *emerge* because of it. The grouping of the notes only *documents* the audible segmentation which is immanent to the notated music. Whether the bar is initially divided unevenly or evenly is noticed by the listener even without knowing the specific notes, namely, on the basis of the tones that represent a higher division level, that is, tones that sound as a third or sixth of the bar, as in the first example, or as quarters of the bar, as in the second example. Also the harmony change inside the bar, that is, a form of the already described aesthetics of the harmony movement, can determine the primary division mode of the bar.

The previous examples present the hierarchical structure of the bar nearly un-exceptionally in the entirely explicit form in which each bar segment of the low-est division level is identifiable by the appearance of a tone. However, the reason for the hierarchical segmentation of the bar does not lie in this explicit form, but *in the principle of the accordance of the bar segments*. The next example shows how even a few representatives of the lowest division level determine the entire segmentation of the bar:

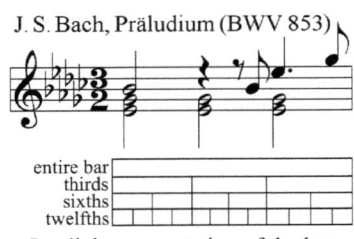

Implicit segmentation of the bar

This bar shows firstly an explicit division of the bar into three segments by three representatives of the first division level. Secondly, two tones appear that represent quarters of such bar thirds, that is, twelfths of the bar. This shows that this bar is, at first, unevenly divided and then, two times, evenly. The validity of the immanent segmentation of the bar for the perception is based on the aesthetic requirement that the bar thirds, firstly, are equably subdivided *in themselves* and, secondly, coincide *among themselves* with regard to their further division. The first third contains therefore four twelfths of the bar, in fact, on the basis of the appearance of the representatives of a division into twelve segments in the further course of the bar.

b) Formation of the Division Levels

The complete segmentation of a bar can, as can be seen, already be indicated by a few tones. On the other hand, the division of the bar is merely as far formed as it is made clear by representatives of the division levels.

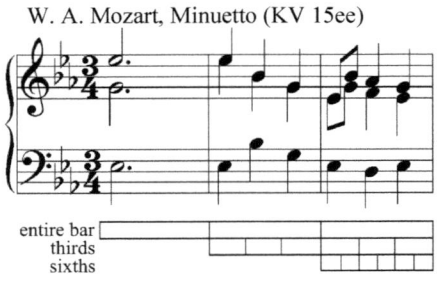

Extension of division levels

In this example, the constitution of the bar segmentation is built up successively, by extending the hierarchy of the division levels in consecutive bars. At the first bar, no subdivision is perceivable yet, at the second bar, the listener notices a division into three parts, at the third bar, a halving of the bar thirds.

However, once a bar segmentation has been set into the world, it remains preserved for subsequent bars even when clear representatives of this segmentation fail to appear. This is because the equable sequence of the harmonies, which makes the bar a standard for subsequent bars, also affects the shaping of the harmonies by subdividing the bar. This subdivision – as a characteristic of the bar – is itself a standard which is determinative for subsequent bars. For a given segmentation of the bar, this involves that it does not have to appear completely in each bar. Because of the general accordance of the bars, a bar segmentation can already constitute itself by clearly occurring in some of the bars. It then achieves a certain stability that remains intact if it is now and then confirmed by correspondingly subdivided bars.

The stability of a bar segmentation can be broken in different ways: A hierarchy of division levels can *form back* if a rougher structure establishes itself as a consistent feature of the bars. However, a bar segmentation can also be *replaced* by a new form of the subdivision. Two cases must be distinguished regarding such a change:

The transition into a new mode of division can be executed *from one bar to the other* if it takes place on a derived level. The following example shows how the transformation of an even division into an uneven division on the third level happens all of a sudden. The uneven division asserts itself so massively within the bar that it instantly displaces the even division of the previous bars. The structural accordance prevailing *within* the bar completes the formation of the new bar segmentation even before the bar has reached its end.

J. S. Bach, Variation 20 (BWV 988), bars 8 and 9

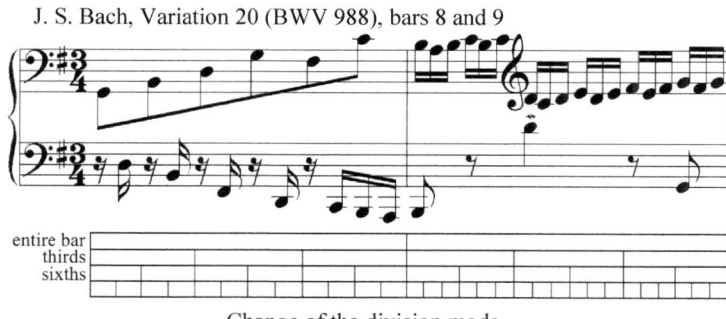

Change of the division mode

For a change of the division mode on the *first* division level, a single bar does not suffice. In such a case, *several bars* of the new division structure have certainly to sound in order for the new structure to constitute itself. Otherwise, the stability of the bar segmentation, which is merely another expression for the general accordance of the bars in reference to their division structure, also affects such bars that do not themselves make any contribution to this segmentation. In this sense, the primary three-part division in the above example is predefined by the preceding bars.

c) Merging of Bar Segments

The hierarchical segmentation of the bar, its equable and more or less continuous partitioning into bar segments, is caused by tones which reveal themselves as products of this partitioning by the moment of their occurrence and by their sound duration. Even with the implicit segmentation of the bar, at least one tone must occur that embodies the result of the division at the lowest division level. Besides, longer tones, embodying higher levels, can also appear, which can even play a role in the formation of bar segmentations if, namely, even and uneven divisions are combined in it. Once the ear has sufficient indications for the perception of a bar segmentation, then this is stabilised by the basic accordance of the bar segments as well as the segmented bars themselves.

On this basis, the sound duration of the tones can also extend across several bar segments, as in the following example:

Merging of three twelfths of the bar

While in this bar the half notes and the eighth notes represent very directly bar thirds and bar twelfths and make them audible, the dotted note (in the circle) unites three twelfths of the bar, or in other words: one sixth and one twelfth of the bar. This tone differs very fundamentally from the other tones in the bar: It does not embody an individual segment of the bar division, but a connection between segments. It makes no contribution to the formation of the bar segmentation, but presupposes its formation as given. It is not involved in the dissection of the bar, but counteracts the separation of the parts by fusing them in its sound duration.

In the musical notation, tones in which bar segments are linked are notated in two different ways: on the one hand, in the very inconspicuous form of a single note, the length of which is determined in relation to the whole note. That this tone is something composite can only be noticed at the bar structure by a closer look. This applies to the above and the following example:

Fusing of two thirds of the bar

On the other hand, in music notation, there is also the highly conspicuous form of visualising such a composite tone by several notes. The notes are then connected by ties in order to indicate the sound unit of the tone. These so-called ligatures are used for various occasions: Either it seems useful to make the bar structure clear for the musician; or the spelling suggests itself due to the audible determinacy of the tone by the bar segmentation; or there is simply no other spelling for the tone in question – as for example in the following bar:

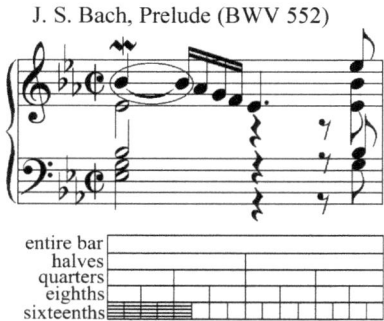

Fusing of five sixteenths of the bar

As a result of the aesthetics of the bar segmentation, the musical tone appears in a further developed shape: The *starting point* of the rhythmic division of the bar is the harmonic bar content, in which the tones are determined as components of harmonies. As the *result* of the bar segmentation, the tones embody bar segments, namely, in two forms: At first, they appear as *separate* bar segments and are, as such, constitutive and bearing elements of the bar structure. This role, they play additionally to their initial role as harmonic components. They constitute bar segmentations even beyond the individual bar and enable thereby the appearance of a second kind of tones which embody a *combination* of bar segments. That which appears as a tone on this derived level *contains* harmonic and rhythmic particles in itself, however, it is neither *identical* with a bar segment nor with a component of a harmony. In this shape, the tone separates itself from its fundamentals and starts playing its own game. During the sounding of such a detached tone, harmonies and even keys can change as the following example shows:

J. S. Bach, Variation 27 (BWV 988), bars 14/15

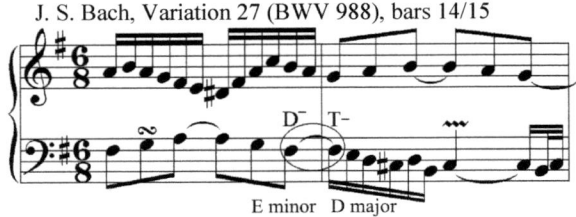

Harmonic metamorphosis of a tone

The tone F sharp which, in the bass of this note example, is tied across the bar line undergoes a harmonic metamorphosis during its sound duration in which it becomes a component not only of changing harmonies, but even of changing keys. At the bar line, namely, a modulation from E minor to D major happens, as can easily be seen by the fact that both bars each contain the entire tone ensemble of their key. In bar 14, the F sharp is a dominant fifth in E minor, then changes its harmonic identity and, in bar 15, ends as a tonic third in D major.

That the components of different keys, when representing adjacent bar segments, can fuse into *one* tone is based on the identity of the tones that makes the keys compatible and their relation harmonious. The keys of E minor and D major have five tones in common which can be tied together in a modulation:

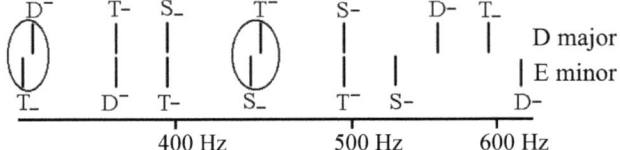

Harmony between E minor and D major

The harmony between the keys is represented here in the form of the so-called pure tone ratios, the way they result immediately from the tonality. In the case of this just intonation, the tones A and E (in the circles) sound in D major by one syntonic comma (81:80) higher than in E minor. The hardly noticeable difference between these tones exists only from the standpoint of the *tonality*. From the standpoint of the *modulation*, the tones in question are each *identical*. In the equally tempered tuning, these tones are not only equated by the perception, but already during the acoustic performance. This *real* equation of the tones shows, when fusing the components of changing keys, its advantage in the fact that it preserves the identity of the tone during its sounding due to a constant tuning.

78

The identity of the tone which is the issue here is of *rhythmic* nature. The tone embodies either one or several bar segments or entire bars. Meanwhile, the term tone appears in a third meaning. The tone that we are now looking at has left behind the identity that it has acquired as a result of the *consonance*: The capacity to sound in different pitches remains reserved for a tone which harmonises with other tones. Only its second ability, resulting from the *modulation*, that is, the ability to perform different harmonic professions in different keys is preserved for the rhythmically determined tone – however, only as a *condition* of its actual determination:

The third abstraction with the name "tone" means a sound form which supports the bar segmentation or reversely is supported by it, that is, which can equally embody a single bar segment as well as the fusion of bar segments. The common characteristic of such tones simply lies in the fact that they sound uninterrupted for a certain duration *at a constant pitch*. That the tone, while sounding, can sound across changes of harmony and is able to take on, one after another, a tonic and a dominant character, that it can even be a representative of changing keys, all of that falls into the range of its *inner preconditions*, which are not immediately apparent in its outer shape. The tone in this definition seems to be so simple that it is frequently regarded as the starting point of the music altogether. In the tonal music, however, it is a very evolved sound figure. A starting point is it only in reference to melodics.

d) Accentuation Ratios

The detachment of the tones from their basis, that is, from the hierarchical bar structure, is also evident in the fact that the bar segmentation as a rhythmic scheme can be perceived and imagined separately. Anyone who whistles a melody when walking, or taps one's foot while listening to music, can separate the sequence of the bar segments from the sequence of the tones. For the perception, the abstract bar segmentation manifests itself in an equable sequence of – imagined or felt – *beats* in the course of the bar. These beats are nothing else than the transitions between the bar segments.

J. S. Bach, Prelude (BWV 1007)

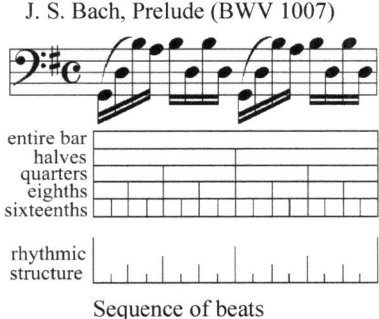

Sequence of beats

79

The music listener also notices that the beats (transitions between the segments) observed within the bar are by no means equivalent, but that more or less weighty beats are permanently alternating. What he perceives as an alternation of heavy and light beats is the temporal sequence of the transitions into bar segments of different division levels. The hierarchy of the divisions appears in the temporal course as a changing valency of the beats with which the bar segments begin. The more segments begin simultaneously, the stronger the beat.

This abstract rhythmic scheme determines the perception of the tones that begin or continue to sound at the moments of the rhythmic beats: The *inner* relationship between the bar segments and their embodiments as tones becomes audible as an *external* relationship between the individual tones and the rank order of the beats hitting them. The tones have, insofar, their rhythmic character by their relation to the abstract bar structure. As such, they have an *accentuation*.

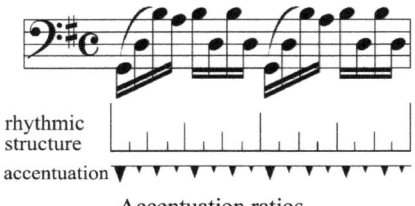

Accentuation ratios

The strongest accentuation is found with those tones that sound at the beginning of a bar. The rhythmic quality of these tones lies in their coincidence with the strong beats that mark the harmony changes. Accordingly, in the above example, the strongest disparity of accentuation results between the first and the second sixteenth notes of the bar.

One can *demonstrate* the accentuation ratios within the bars by *emphasising* them when making music. The accentuation itself which is the matter here exists, however, independently of any emphasising, which is possible with most musical instruments. It is also perceivable in the case of a completely equable intonation, such as can be achieved, for instance, on barrel organs or computers. More accentuated or stressed tones do not mean louder tones, and accentuation in music is not the same as accentuation in speech. The fact that the accentuation is based on the bar segmentation and not on performance manners is strikingly revealed in the case of rests that begin with strong beats and therefore coincide with weighty bar segments. These rests are perceived as *suppressed* accentuations.

J. S. Bach, Fugue (BWV 581)

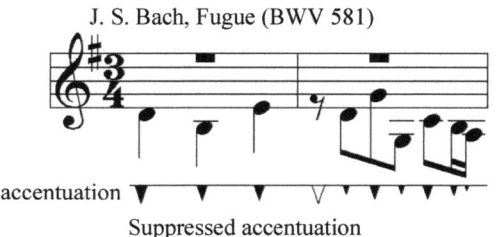

Suppressed accentuation

The accentuation is a *property* of the tone. Certainly, this property exists only in the relation to other tones, as a *relative* accentuation, and even that only on the basis of the segmentation of the bar; but nevertheless, it *adheres* to the tone itself. If this tone embodies several merged bar segments, more or less weighty beats compete for the privilege of determining the accentuation of the tone in question. The outcome of this competition is always the same: It is always decided by the weight of the biggest beat that falls into the sound of the tone. There are two different cases: The weightier beat can coincide with the beginning of the tone or fall into the time frame of the tone already sounding.

W. A. Mozart, Minuetto (KV 15y)

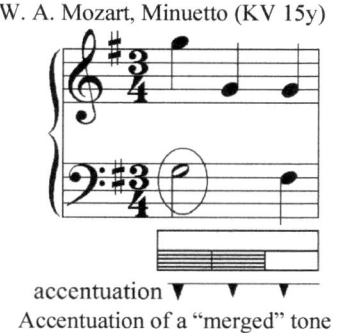

accentuation

Accentuation of a "merged" tone

In the above case, the half note in the bass represents a fusion of the first and second thirds of the bar. Two beats fall into the sound of this tone: The big beat, which coincides with the beginning of the bar, and the small one, which separates the second third of the bar from the first one. When the tone begins to sound, it has – just like the quarter note in the upper voice – the strongest accentuation in the bar, namely the accentuation of the first bar third. At this point, the stress in the lower voice does not differ from that in the upper voice. Things are different in the second bar third: Now the upper voice has the lighter accentuation of the second bar third, while the lower voice *retains* the accentuation that the tone has from the beginning. For the tone in the bass, the second beat is therefore powerless against the first beat, which asserts itself with all the weight of its position at the beginning of the bar. The tone, which can have only *one* accentuation, thus retains the weight of its accentuation and makes the second beat ineffective. The situation is different in the case of a *syncope*.

In the case of a syncope, the bigger beat falls into the already sounding tone. Such a tone does not show its accentuation already at the beginning of its sounding, but only when the stronger beat falls into its sounding. However, since the accentuation is a quality which belongs to the tone *as a whole*, that is, even then when it begins to sound, the perception allocates the beginning of this accentuation *retroactively* to the moment at which the tone starts. For the perception, therefore, the accentuation appears *relocated*, back to a moment where it could not have been noticed yet. This ability of the perception to retroactively position the beginning of a perceived sound figure has already been demonstrated several times: The change of a harmony or a key, its taking place or not taking place at the beginning or in the middle of a bar, all this is only noticed afterwards.

A. Bredon/J. Page/R. Plant, Babe I'm Gonna Leave You (1969)

accentuation

Syncope

The syncope is therefore a tone whose accentuation appears shifted. In the above example, the syncope already *occurs* during the *fourth* eighth of the bar with an accentuation that actually only *originates* from the *fifth* eighth, that is, from the transition into the second bar half. The rhythmic effect of the syncope is all the more drastic the larger the imbalance is between the beats at the beginning and during the sounding of a tone. The strongest syncopes are therefore always those that sound across a bar line.

A correct definition of the syncope, aiming at the essence of the matter, could be this: A syncope is a tone in which a bar segment is merged with at least one subsequent bar segment which occupies a higher position in the hierarchy of the bar segments. In musicology and in the musical practice, definitions have prevailed which are useful for the identification of syncopes only because they are oriented towards the necessary outward appearance of the syncope: If one designates the relative accentuation peculiar to the bar segments as *bar value*, then the syncope appears as a *"rhythmic shift by binding a not accentuated value to the following accentuated one"*. And if one considers the contrast between the accentuation of a tone and that of its first bar value, then the syncope appears as *"the accentuation of a not accentuated bar value"*.

From the theoretical analysis so far, it is evident on what the sensibility of the music listener for accentuations is based: first, on the intuitive grasp of the aesthetics which lies in the equability of the harmonic movement; second, on the feeling for the accordance of the segments that result from a consecutive division of the bars. The perception takes the kind of the division quite unconsciously and naturally from the indications that the music offers for this, and assigns all sounding tones to the emerging bar structure. Consequently, this result comes about without any knowledge about how and why this comes about, and even without the awareness that this is about a result. The *segments* formed from the bar can, conversely, even be considered as *elements* that the bar is made from, without this misconception having any influence on the music or its enjoyment.

The accentuation ratios in the bar are a conspicuous phenomenon. They therefore offer an important aid to orientation for the musical practice, for the performance of concerts, and for writing down sheet music. In fact, the bar lines are usually not found by looking at the harmonies, but by searching for the strongest accents. Therefore, the illusion readily arises that the accentuation ratios are not only in practice but also in substance the starting point from which the bar results. How this popular inversion of cause and effect has attained honours even in musicology is yet to be illuminated in a little more detail at the end of this chapter.

e) Harmonic Contrast

The tones that are dispersed in the bar with different accentuations have only their *external* correlation in that. *Internally*, they are first and foremost interrelated as components of harmonies and underlie the musical bar in precisely this definition. The manner, however, how the tones occur in the bar has definitely an influence on their weight as harmonic components and, hence, on the characteristic of the harmony itself.

The stronger or weaker presence of a tone in the bar can depend on various factors. A tone has relatively more weight under the following conditions:

- It sounds in a lower register, provides more partials, has more sound mass.
- It sounds in different octave positions, and that also possibly at the same time.
- It is played louder (for example by a louder instrument).
- It sounds longer than other tones.
- It occurs more frequently in the bar.
- It has an accent as a reflex of the bar segmentation.

The last point is particularly important here.

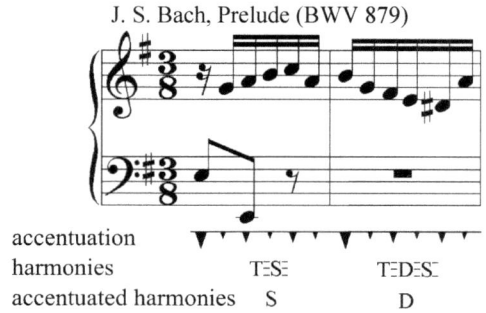

J. S. Bach, Prelude (BWV 879)

Main and secondary tones of the harmonies

The above two bars contain dissonances of the key of E minor. However, if the focus is only on the tones that, in their accentuation, mark the three-part division of the bar, then a sequence of a subdominant and dominant appears as the core of the harmonic motion. A musician would therefore intuitively accept these harmonies as the adequate accompaniment on an additional instrument. The un-

83

accented harmonic components are, by contrast, only perceived as a nuancing of the actual harmonies.

The distinction between main and secondary tones, which comes about in the way in which a bar content is shaped, opens up new spaces for the harmony movement: Bars with identical content, which – in extreme cases – comprise the complete tone ensemble of a key, can nevertheless follow one another as distinguishable harmonies. The harmonies can namely differ in the tonal characteristic of those sound components on which the main weight in the bar lies. The laws of tonality and modulation are not affected by this. They are valid independently of the weight that the tones have in the bar. But the harmony change, which is the basis of the bar, can take place as a change of the harmonic main emphasis.

f) The Thorough Bass Era

The periodic harmony change contained in the concept of the bar *presupposes* the definiteness and the contrast of the harmonies. Both, however, definitely also *come about* the other way round by the bar and its shapings: Firstly, the bar includes a determination of the temporal frame for the harmonies, thereby defining the belonging together of the harmonic components, and is consequently involved in the shaping of harmonies and tonal transitions, as the analysis in the previous chapter has already shown. Secondly, it has now turned out that the, in the bar findable, distribution of the weights, where accentuation ratios also play a role, influence the contrast of the harmonies. Music as a sequence of bars, the self-stabilising evenness of the harmonic movement, must, on the other hand, have originated on a basis which has *not* yet developed from the bar itself.

This "big bang" of the tonal music is relatively easy to reconstruct as it dates back only a few centuries and has left its mark over a period of several decades. The period of the genesis of the bar stretched over the entire 17th century and coincides with a musical era for which Hugo Riemann has coined the adequate term "the age of figured bass". During this era the style of the basso continuo dominated. The music was based on an equably continuous sequence of chords, which were put over a tone sequence in the bass. The basso continuo was popular as a concert accompaniment, but also as an independent music style. The corresponding notation of the figured (thorough) bass consisted in the fixation of the bass notes under which the chords to be played were indicated by figures.

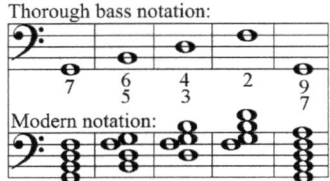

Figured bass notation and its realisation in notes

What was epoch-making about the style of the basso continuo was that it made the sequence of harmonies a starting point for the composing of music. It reversed the standpoint that the old counterpoint doctrines took on the harmonies, it treated the harmonies not only as a mere condition to be taken into account for the purpose of a passable voice leading, but as something that should be crucial in music and on which it could be firmly based. And it was precisely therein that the basso continuo already created an archaic form of the bar.[1]

The figured bass notation only fixed the harmony as such, but not by any means the form of its realisation. The practical procedure corresponded insofar to the logical relation between the bar and bar segmentation. The musician was supposed to form and ornament the harmonies according to taste, imagination, intuition, and fashion. Depending on experience and exercise, he was able to present the bar content in ever bolder shapes. The experience showed that the insertion of non-notated tones at unaccented points did not stand in contradiction to the orientation towards the written figured bass. In this way, a separation of main and secondary tones was formed.

The harmonic and rhythmic character of the music finally became so natural that it also came about in free improvisations. With this result, however, the figured bass has rendered its own starting point to be superfluous: With the introduction of the bar, it was no longer necessary to conceive the music on the basis of outlined harmonies.[2] The need arose to attach more importance to the way in which the harmonies were to be structured and presented and to make them visible in notes, that is, to translate the figured bass into modern notation. The music that was now to be notated had a rhythmic character in principle, and the introduction of the bar line at the beginning of the 18th century took this fact into account. However, this, in general, led to the emergence of the modern notation, which is based on the bar and which can also be called the notation of the tonal music.

---

[1] *"The* sestina *cycle ... is Monteverdi's last set of madrigals without a thoroughbass. A conspicuous feature of the first madrigal,* Incenerite spoglie, *is the slow and uniform 'harmonic rhythm', that is, the time intervals between changes of chord ... The measure thus forms the unit of harmonic motion."* (Carl Dahlhaus, *Studies on the Origin of Harmonic Tonality*, trans. Robert O. Gjerdingen, Princeton 1990, pp. 307 f.)

[2] Nevertheless, as Forkel reports, J. S. Bach demanded extensive exercises in the art of figured bass from his students in order to develop their feeling for harmonic motion sequences before all attempts at composing: *"Bach's method of teaching composition was equally sure and effective ... He did not begin with the dry details of counterpoint, as was the custom of other teachers in his day. Still less did he burden his pupils with the physical properties of sound, which he held to be matter for the theorist and instrument-maker rather than the composer. He started them off at once on four-part harmony over a figured Bass, making his pupils write each part on a separate stave in order to impress on them the need for accurate harmonic progression."* (Johann Nikolaus Forkel, *Johann Sebastian Bach. His Life, Art and Work*, trans. Charles Sanford Terry, New York 1920, p. 85)

The fact that the emergence of the bar is related to the development of the tonality is, by the way, also noticed by authors who *do not* know the reason for this, namely the *logical* relationship between bar and tonality:

"Bar rhythmics and harmonic tonality began to consolidate – as it seems, in interdependence of each other." [1]

What is internally connected, however, can very well fall apart externally, as the modern development and use of percussion instruments show. These initially serve for the underlining of the bar structure, yet, as elaborate percussion instruments, they also increasingly make an own contribution to the constitution of the bar segmentation. Finally, they continue their work while the other instruments pause and thereby they achieve a detachment of the bar from its harmonic basis. A drum solo presents beat sequences, which are, so to speak, based on abstract bars, that is, on equably following and hierarchically segmented time units, which can even be perceived as such without a harmonic content and therefore without the marking changes of harmony. That these "abstract" bars are also based on the tonal music and fit in with it, is little noticed. Abstract rhythms are, conversely, a popular argument to underpin the illusion that the musical bar is actually determined abstractly from the ground up and that the harmonic content is something that can be added afterwards in order to fill out the bar that is supposed to exist separately from the harmonic motion.

The fact that abstract rhythms existed even before the emergence of the tonal music is usually taken as a confirmation of this false conception of the bar. In doing so, the fact is ignored that the rhythms of the modal music were not yet determined by a bar at all. These rhythms, which, until recently, could still be documented by ethnomusicologists in reserves of the modal music, not only originated in religious psalm verses, but were also practiced with the help of mnemotechnic verses. A hierarchical segmentation of given time units was not only unknown, but was already excluded by the number of syllables of a verse, which often represented a prime number (11, 13, 17, 19 or 37). From the standpoint of the tonal music, these rhythms appear "irrational", and are also occasionally referred to as such today. In the case of these rhythms, there was no bar dissected into segments, but, conversely, a number of elements was put together into a group.[2] In the following, it will be seen that it has obviously become usual in modern musicology to confuse tonal rhythmics with modal rhythmics by misunderstanding the bar as a group of given elements.

---

[1] Carl Dahlhaus and Hans Heinrich Eggebrecht (eds.), *Brockhaus Riemann Musiklexikon*, vol. 4, Mainz 1998, p. 44.

[2] Further details in: Franz Sauter, *Die Musikwissenschaft in Forschung und Lehre. Kritik einer bürgerlichen Wissenschaft*, Norderstedt 2010, pp. 181-209, in particular the annotations about the rhythmics of modal music using the examples of the Indian ganas (pp. 196 f.) and the Arabic wazn (pp. 205 f.).

g) Theories About the Bar

Modern musical notation characterises the bar structure by indications of how many notes of a certain length form the bar. These indications assume note lengths which are not defined as parts of the bar, but as parts of the whole note. Thereby the semblance arises as if the bar is not the logical starting point of its division, but, conversely, the result of a putting together of presupposed elements. Music theories usually proclaim this mistake before their readers as a very substantial knowledge.[1] Hugo Riemann's definition of the bar as *"the smallest higher unit to which several counting times convene"* circulates in musicology as a holy revelation,[2] where, in the gesture of precise definition, it is pretended as if *"higher units"* out of *"counting times"* are something real in music, which one can arrange according to size, only in order to find out the bar as the smallest of these units, and not possibly the bar half, which is admittedly even smaller, but not a *"higher unit"*, as one can see from the definition of the bar ...

In a downright classical way, Hugo Riemann endeavoured, in all seriousness, to clarify that ominous construct of a time unit which is imagined as the elementary form of the rhythmical and for which, for this very reason, the derivation from the division of the bar is ruled out. His first step into the issue consists in confusing his musical subject with the problems of chronometry:

"»Time itself does not divide at all, rather it requires for the purpose of the segmentation of the temporal progression something (sensuously perceptible) other that carries it out.« This basic statement by Aristoxenos (Rhythm. p. 272), which flatly refuses the definition of a rhythm in itself without reference to a something that is rhythmised, still rightly persists today. The same" [this statement] *"dispels, once and for all, all attempts to declare naked schemes of the division of the time into fractions of equal duration as foundations of a viable and fruitful rhythmical theory."* [3]

The sentence of Aristoteles' student Aristoxenos concerns, however much it is meant to be a contribution to the theory of rhythm, a topic of physics, which, however, knows more suitable periodic processes for the defining of time units than music can ever provide.[4] By this sentence, Riemann intends in no way to

---

[1] An example of this mistake: *"The rhythmic main value (counting time, counting unit, beat) is a time unit which represents the basic element of a bar ... The bar is formed by grouping several rhythmic main values whereby a superordinate unit, out of a certain number of these elements with a set duration, emerges."* (Erich Wolf, *Allgemeine Musiklehre*, Wiesbaden 1967, p. 57)

[2] For example, cited in: Wolf, *Allgemeine Musiklehre*, p. 56, or in: Hermann Grabner, *Allgemeine Musiklehre*, Kassel 1974, p. 35.

[3] Hugo Riemann, *System der musikalischen Rhythmik und Metrik*, Leipzig 1903, p. 1.

[4] *"In order to define a time unit, any periodic process can basically be used."* (Oscar Höfling, *Physik. Lehrbuch für Unterricht und Selbststudium*, Bonn 1985, p. 20). Höfling means *natural* processes and explains that in the case of time measuring it is a question of eliminating as many interfering influences as possible on an applied periodicity.

"dispel" the misconception that the musical rhythm is in any form a matter of time division. Quite the contrary. On the other hand, he is neither interested in time division in a rational way by *undertaking* this with the help of knowledge about periodic processes, and by defining time units. He is, conversely, in search of a priori *existing* time units, which function as rhythmic elements in music and insofar establish periodic processes. He looks for *"a something"* like the legendary "rhythmizomenon" of Aristoxenos, and, in fact, he looks for it in the human nature:

"The scientific finding of the last principle of the rhythm through Karl Bücher's study »Labour and Rhythm«, which rightly caused a stir, has brought a substantial clarification ... Bücher has, to an enhanced degree, directed the attention to the general importance of the conscious adherence to an equable division of time for the economy of our power development and, above all, pointed out that the essence of rhythm is by no means necessarily of sonic nature." [1]

Riemann not only finds his time unit independently of observing the music, but can even give more precise information on how long it lasts:

"Detailed experiments indeed reveal a quite narrowly limitable middle in which the temporal distance of sensuously perceived successional appearances is described by all people as neither fast nor slow; ... J. Fr. Herbart, who was the first to emphasise the fundamental importance of such a mean value for the assessment of the tempo of successional appearances, determined the same to about one second; we may, based on the results of repeated thorough examinations, determine the same more precisely to about little less than ¾ of a second, namely approx. 75 - 80 per minute ... By determining the normal mean time value, from where we evaluate all sensuously perceptible successional appearances as slow or fast, it is given to us the first foundation on which the essence of the rhythm is based." [2]

Where Riemann comes back to the music again, it becomes, as if by itself, the "content" of his time units, which, thereby, in turn remain spared from the unfruitful existence as *"naked schemata"* and only thereby become truly real:

"The counting times (beat times, rhythmic basic times) gain real existence under any circumstances only by their contents." [3]

Riemann, who believes that his idea of time units corresponds to a musical reality as soon as he additionally thinks of a musical content, wants to explain the accentuation relations on this theoretical basis, but at least notices that the assumption of an accentuated *time unit* is not a self-evident thought:

"In itself, the distinction of the successive time units in important and less important ones or, as one would say: heavy and light ones, is certainly, by no means, a self-evident thing." [4]

---

[1] Riemann, *System der musikalischen Rhythmik und Metrik*, p. 3.

[2] Ibid., pp. 4 ff.

[3] Ibid., p. 8.

[4] Ibid., p. 8.

In a mysterious way, this distinction nevertheless becomes a self-evident thing for him, and, in fact, only in that he imagines the time units as being real and filled with a musical content:

"... as a content of a unit forming the pulse beat of the rhythm, a majority of perceptible phenomena (that is for the music: intonations) has, in principle, to be assumed. This majority, however, entails without further ado the distinction of the weight." [1]

Riemann's theoretical successors see no problem either in associating the accentuation relations with the curious elementary particles from which they derive the bar:

"The bar summarises a certain group of counting times, considering the accentuation ratios." [2]

Accordingly, the accentuation ratios relate to the bar as follows: They are being *"considered"* when summarising the counting times, that is, they are somehow already there before this summarising.

Similarly, Grabner does not see the accentuation ratios as something that he would have to explain, but as something that has to be observed and fixed in writing. He writes a melody *without* bar lines and remarks the following about it:

"If one sings this melody, the striving to organise these tones in a periodic recurring manner stands out immediately and, in doing so, to subject certain tones to a stronger accentuation. This is done by dividing it into bars. It is carried out by the so-called bar line, which combines the counting times belonging together and, at the same time, fixes the distribution of the main emphases." [3]

Grabner does not go about analysing this melody in order to find the reason for the singers' observed behaviour. He does not assume at all that this behaviour could have an *objective* reason in the sung melody. Instead, he believes that the singers have a *subjective* reason, independent of the real melody, to emphasise certain tones. He grasps the accentuation ratios only as an *activity* of accentuating. And he considers the objective existence of the bar lines to be a *means* of carrying out this subjective activity. He offers a *tautology* as the reason for this general human behaviour: The human strives to bring a certain order into the melody so that it takes an orderly course:

"By regulating the value ratios of the individual tones among each other and by setting the tempo, the possibility of an orderly course of the melody seems to be sufficiently given." [4]

In Grabner's opinion, the *explanation* of the bar is equivalent to the statement that the bar is *useful* by satisfying a human need for order. – Once the sense of order has been identified as the cause of the bar, one can assume that the bar is at

[1] Riemann, System der musikalischen Rhythmik und Metrik, p. 9.

[2] Wieland Ziegenrücker, *Allgemeine Musiklehre*, Mainz 1982, p. 38.

[3] Grabner, *Allgemeine Musiklehre*, p. 35.

[4] Ibid., p. 34.

work quite independently of the music and can supposedly even be heard in the case of the *"ticking of a clock"*, as another author teaches us:

"If we hear a series of regularly consecutive beats, e.g. the ticking of a clock, then our ear has the striving to summarise these beats into groups of several units. This striving for an ordering summarisation, we not only have for the smallest, but for the superimposed larger units as well. Such equal groups of units repeating themselves regularly in compositions are indicated by vertical lines. We call the delimited units bars, the lines delimiting them bar lines." [1]

The theory of the time units lives by the idea that the tones are combined in the bar *for the sake of good order*. This idea is not based on an analysis of the bar, but on an ideological preference, on the desire for an orderly course of all things. This beautiful principle literally cries out for manifold proofs for its worldwide existence so that there is still a wide task field waiting for generations of researchers:

"The biological rhythm research starts out from the observation that the whole world, macro- and microcosm, moves periodically ..." [2]

Now that we know that the universe is already full of harmony and rhythm, we can be curious whether at least the melody will remain in the music ...

---

[1] Kurt Johnen, *Allgemeine Musiklehre*, Stuttgart 1999, pp. 14 f.

[2] Wilhelm Seidel, *Rhythmus. Eine Begriffsbestimmung*, Darmstadt 1976, p. 6.

III. Melodics

6. Aesthetics of Scale Degree Relations

a) Transformation of Tonal Relations into Intervals

The starting point of all melodic structures is the *rhythmically defined tone*. This is not that abstract tone which, as a component of harmonies, also underlies the rhythm and in terms of which it is negligible at what pitch, at which position, how frequently, and how long it sounds in the bar. Rather, the matter here is the concrete, in the bar individualised, tone whose position, extension, and sonic existence is immediately based on the bar segmentation. However, the property, which opens the door to new aesthetic dimensions for this tone, is, in turn, very abstract: It is its, for a shorter or longer duration, uninterrupted sounding in a certain pitch.

Tones of this kind relate to each other according to the criterion of their pitch. They compare themselves after their tone pitch and match all the more the closer they lie together. On this basis, the tone ensembles of the keys transform into musical *scales*, and the tonal relations into *scale degree ratios* or, what is the same, into *intervals*. These basic forms of the melodic shall now be analysed closer, the more so as they are usually not considered to be derived forms at all.

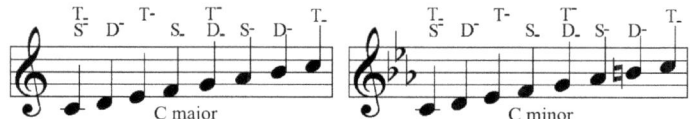

Scales in major and minor

The scale, at first, has the peculiarity that, in it, the tones of a key are strung together according to their pitch level, that is, in an order in which the harmonic determinacy and belonging together of the tones is quite hidden. The tonic, dominant, and subdominant seem to have been jumbled and are hardly recognisable as what they represent in the cadence in a readily apparent manner. Nevertheless, these harmonies do have their effect and create tonality so that, in the above tone scales, the last tone appears in each case as a resolution of the previously accumulated dissonance. The cause of this effect, however, hides behind the superficial form of the progression on scale degrees.

The harmonic difference between major and minor keys appears in the scales as a specific succession of different distances between immediately successive tone degrees. These distances between the scale degrees result from the harmonic relation between the tonal components, or more specifically: from the frequency ratios in which the tonal relations manifest itself. From the determinations developed in the second chapter, the following "pure" frequency ratios between the degrees can be calculated:

Degrees:	1.	2.	3.	4.	5.	6.	7.	8.
Major:	9:8	10:9	16:15	9:8	10:9	9:8	16:15	
Minor:	9:8	16:15	10:9	9:8	16:15	75:64	16:15	

On the basis of the aesthetics of the modulation, the syntonic comma (81:80) between the whole tones 9:8 and 10:9 can be neglected, and exactly that is indeed the handling of the tones in the case of the equal temperament. Hence, the harmonic structure inherent to a musical scale presents itself as an order in which the minor, major and augmented second (75:64) – or semitone, whole tone and, if you will, "one and a half tone" – occur:

Major:	1	1	½	1	1	1	½
Minor:	1	½	1	1	½	1½	½

In which distances scale degrees occur, that is a purely *harmonic* matter, which is the predefined basis of the specific arrangement of the scale degrees. Since when singing the tone pitches within a key are hit because of the harmonic intuition, the distances between the degrees can, in practice, be presupposed as given with the utmost naturalness. To some music theorists, this naturalness does not reveal the harmonic basis of the scale degrees, the law of tonality, but rather an arbitrarily arisen tradition preserved by pure imitation, which can and have to be abandoned for the purpose of freeing the music.[1]

The pitch level comparison, schematised in the musical scales, logically does not define what is compared, that is, no *tone pitches*, but *scale degrees*. The pitches are already predefined by the tone ensembles of the keys, and that across all audible octave spaces so that they are available as a material of an arbitrarily up- and downwardly extendable scale. What characterises the tone degrees themselves is expressed by ordinal numbers: Counted from the tonic root tone – that is, from the keytone –, there is a first, second, third etc. level, and these designations refer so solidly to the predetermined harmonic tone relations that they can be used for the description of harmonies. For example, the term "triad of the fourth scale degree", which is based on melodic ideas, is always clearly to be understood as a name for what is harmonically characterised as the subdominant. However, that the, in such conventions contained, semblance of a melodic basis of the harmonies is then theoretically taken deadly seriously is something that the degree designations of the chords bear no blame for.

---

[1] The common distinction between harmonic and melodic minor scales does not want to know anything about the fact that the modern scale is always the *melodic* form of a *harmonic* constellation. What is presented in this context as a melodic minor scale and what is supposed to consist of other tones in the downward movement than in the upward movement is a construct that has neither something to do with tonal keys nor with scales.

On the basis of the scale degrees, the harmonic tone relations take on a completely new form. After these relations have, already in the frequency ratios, an external manifestation distinguishable from their inner harmony, they now additionally transform into intervals, whose size is measured by how many degrees they span. According to this, the intervals are named: Beginning from an arbitrary tone, a further tone lies

- as a prime   on the *same* level
- as a second   on the *next* level
- as a third   on the *third* level
- as a fourth   on the *fourth* level
- as a fifth   on the *fifth* level etc.

One can now see the, in melodic ideas based, origin of the names, which also have found its way into the harmonic terminology. By the way, also the musical notation is based on the degree relations of the melodics so that an abstract tone mentioned by name such as the tone A becomes very concrete as soon as it is notated on one or the other stave line.

Intervals are different by their size. Sevenths and octaves may differ harmonically as dissonance and consonance; as intervals, they are just different in size. But "size" always means, in the case of intervals, the distance between the tones *measured in scale degrees*. That is why the minor third and the augmented second are different intervals, "although", seen in isolation, they sound equally. Remarkable is also the form in which intervals *do not* differ: All intervals between consecutive degrees are of the same size. Regardless of all harmonic differences, and therefore also regardless of all differences between the minor, major, and augmented second, all seconds match as intervals by definition. Likewise, all thirds, all fourths etc. All aesthetics and accordance in melodics are based on this identity of the intervals.

b) Concept of the Melody

The intervals are a further type of tone relations aside from the ones dealt with so far: The tones not only *harmonise* as consonant and dissonant bar contents as well as components of changing keys, they not only have *rhythmic* relations as representatives of bar segments and thereby as accentuation bearers, but also compare themselves according to their pitch. The aesthetics of the scale degree relations resulting from this is realised in the melody.

The tones of a melody relate to each other as successive representatives of degrees of an underlying scale. The melody is thus a sequence of tones which are connected to each other by intervals. For a melodic tone, it is crucial whether it sounds on the same degree as its predecessor, whether it sounds higher or lower, and if so, how many scale degrees there are between the tones. It is in the *sequence of intervals* that the connection between the melodic tones and thus the identity of the melody lies.

One can also express this peculiarity of the melodic in a more flowery fashion by the common metaphor in which the tone is presented as a being that moves on the steps of a scale like a boisterous child. According to this catchy convention of speech, the tone moves in the melody in smaller or larger leaps up- or downwards, progresses on the same level or remains there for a shorter or longer while, interrupts its motion occasionally by rests, thus moving, for example, in the following way:

J. S. Bach, Fugue (BWV 535)

Melodic tone sequence

As far as the German term "Tonbewegung" ("tone motion") expresses metaphorically that the melodic tones are referred to each other by intervals, this term is quite appropriate, and it does not matter that the tone, which is defined in this chapter by its individual pitch, yet again comes along in a different meaning and maintains its identity as a tone throughout the entire course of "its" motion, in which it constantly changes its pitch. The only thing wrong is the mysticism which wants to deduce the "tone motion", quite seriously, from "motion energies" and "force fields":

"Music is ... a temporal progression. This one appears to the listener as an experience of a movement process which has its root in the motion energy inherent in each tone sequence ... That is also suggested by many expressions which we use in music: "step", "leap", "run", ... It is this motion energy that puts every tone in a certain balance of power in relation to the others and gives it a functional meaning for the overall course." [1]

Linguistic formulations do not prove facts, but express the matter that is to be clarified more or less adequately, at best. That they otherwise can also inspire the imagination is undisputed. But conversely, a vivid imagination can also lead to special linguistic creations. One of these is the "leading tone" treated in the following.

c) The Myth of the Leading Tone

If one observes the harmonic movement, the constant build-up of the harmonic tension between the subdominant and dominant and its harmonic resolution into the tonic, from the melodic side, then this movement appears in the form of *intervals* in which the transition into the tonic takes place over and over again. This *form* of the movement is therefore, when superficially viewed, easily considered to be the *matter itself* so that the reasons for the consequence noticeable in the

---

[1] Hermann Grabner, *Allgemeine Musiklehre*, Kassel 1974, pp. 57 f.

appearance of the tonic are searched for *in the melodic movement*. They lie, according to the quite unanimous opinion of music theorists, in the nature of the semitone step, in which a secret "striving" is assumed.

Semitone steps in the scales

Referred to the above example, the view is established in the world of music that, in both scales, the tone B "strives" towards the tone C. Many also believe that, in the case of the minor scale, the tone D "strives" towards the tone E flat, especially when this semitone step is seen in the context of a polyphonic music piece. As soon as the tones are observed in reversed order, that is, in a downwards directed scale, many theorists discover in the above major scale a further "striving" from F to E, and in the minor scale from A flat to G. Hence, they differentiate between an upwards and downwards directed "striving". Strangely enough, the question of whether a tone "strives" towards another one, and even whether it "strives" upwards or downwards, depends on whether the "target tone" of this "striving" is a tone of the tonic or not. From this, however, the theorists draw no conclusion about the character of the tonic, about its determination as the harmonic resolution of a harmonic contrast, but about a "forwarding energy", which they so certainly assume to be in a preceding tone that they call it a *leading tone*.

"Like the Greek scale, also our major scale is composed of two tetrachords (= four tone series ...) ... The course of the upward striving motion appears, furthermore, divided into two phases by the endpoint of the first and the starting point of the second tetrachord. Important is now the observation that, before the target tones (...), a sharp compression of the motion energy in the form of the semitones ... occurs. We call such tones in which a particularly strong forwarding energy is inherent which absolutely urges forward into a resolution into the end tone of the phase 'leading tones'. They are always semitones ..." [1]

The strange thing about this energy that is compressed *"in the form of semitones"* is above all this: Without the *"target tone"* into which the *"forwarding energy"* urges, there is no semitone at all, which, by the way, is an interval between *two* tones even if this is a bit forgotten in the statement that *"such tones ... are always semitones"*. The interval between two successive tones is said to have the power to bring about its own realisation. The occurrence of a tone is supposed to be caused by the relation that *it* has to the preceding tone, in which relation, however, its occurrence is already logically presupposed. Every definition of the *'leading tone'* is a tautology of this calibre.

---

[1] Grabner, *Allgemeine Musiklehre*, pp. 58 f.

*"**Leading tone** [...], a tone leading to another, stimulating the same one in the state of expectancy, which preferably lies a semitone below the tonic, e.g. B in C major. The step from the leading tone to the target tone is always a minor second ... Its forward-directed tendency is melodically to be explained by the small distance to the following tone, harmonically by the belonging to a mostly dominant sound."* [1]

This definition, which takes into account the difference between tone and interval, claims that *"the small distance to the following tone"* causes a tendency towards exactly this following tone. The *"target tone"* is stimulated *"in the state of expectancy"* on the basis of a distance which already presupposes its existence. The fact that harmonic aspects are also brought into play does not alter the absurdity of the definition. The assertion that an imaginary construct like the leading note is to be explained equally melodically and harmonically does not testify to a theoretical interest in the connection between harmonic and melodic forms. In a similar way, the following explanation of the leading tone mentions two causes for the supposed fact that this one resolves itself into a different tone:

*"**Leading tone**: a tone which, by its melodic or harmonic meaning, strives towards a resolution into another tone. The leading tone and the target tone are always a semitone step apart from each other. The direction of movement is ascending or descending ... The most important leading tone is the 7th tone of the scale, which resolves itself towards the 8th degree, the root tone. This leading tone is, at the same time, the third of the dominant, which, for its part, as a striving sound, targets the tonic."* [2]

The author cannot make up his mind whether a harmonic or melodic *"meaning"* of the leading tone is fundamental. For example, he does not care how the melodic determination of a tone as the seventh tone of the scale relates to its harmonic determination as a tone of the dominant. In his opinion, these are merely equivalent angles from which the matter can be viewed. And also the observed thing itself – whether the tone ascends or descends – is mentioned just as indifferently and incoherently as the *"melodic or harmonic meaning"* attributed to the movement. Only one thing is beyond doubt in his opinion: *"The leading tone and the target tone are always a semitone step apart from each other."* These tones only exist in a semitone distance, and at the same time, they are supposed to bring about the realisation of a semitone step.

Apart from that, the characterisation of the dominant as a "striving sound" follows the same pattern as the construct of a leading tone: The dominant is presented as a sound which "strives" towards the tonic because of its relation to exactly this following tonic. However, it only has this striving if the tonic actually follows. The occurrence of the tonic is ultimately always explained by the fact

---

[1] Carl Dahlhaus and Hans Heinrich Eggebrecht (eds.), *Brockhaus Riemann Musiklexikon*, vol. 3, Mainz 1998, p. 28.

[2] Gerhard Kwiatkowski et al. (eds.), *Meyers kleines Lexikon Musik*, Mannheim et al. 1986, p. 197.

that it occurs. The right explanation has been given in the second chapter of this book: The harmonic consequence that is a feature of the tonic in its appearance as the resolution is based on the occurrence of the dominant *and* subdominant. Because the harmonic relation between *these* sounds presupposes – not the appearance of the tonic, but: – the *mediation* by a sound that is *exactly thereby* defined as a tonic. That is why the musician is intuitively able to identify the sound in which the definition of the tonic is realised. He can identify the tonic on the basis of the harmonic confrontation of the counter sounds, and he can anticipate it in his imagination.

The following explanation of the leading tone is remarkable because it *deals with* the relation between the harmonic and melodic form – and turns it upside down:

"The third of the dominant triad has ... a melodic meaning of its own kind. It is the 7th step of the scale, hence, it precedes the tonic in the melodic succession of the scale and leads over into it. Only a semitone step apart from the tonic, the 7th level obtains the character of a leading tone to the tonic, i.e. of a tone in which the sharply pronounced tendency is identifiable to transition into the tonic, to resolve itself into the tonic. The fact that the leading tone belongs to the dominant chord as its third is now also co-determining for the harmonic relation of the dominant to the tonic." [1]

The leading tone, this chimera of a tone that, in the semitone step which it tends to carry out, at the same time possesses the cause of this tendency, is, according to this, supposed to effect the resolution into the tonic. By a curious coincidence, the leading tone belongs to a harmony that already is in a relation to the tonic anyway because of the harmonic law of the tonality. The authors are not able to bring this *harmonic* relationship into any connection with the resolution into the tonic, for which they instead want to know solely a *melodic* reason. However, they can well imagine that the alleged melodic tendency of the leading tone "co-determines" a harmonic relationship.

By the way, the talk of the "meaning" of the most diverse sound figures that appears in the last quotations, but also everywhere else in musicology, is extremely inappropriate from a factual point of view. Chords, tones, tone sequences and so on have certain properties and stand in certain relations, but they do not mean anything.[2] Since the contrary opinion bases its evidences on phenomena

---

[1] Rudolf Louis and Ludwig Thuille, *Harmonielehre*, Stuttgart 1907, p. 4.

[2] *"Stories are not what music means. Music is never* about *things. Music just* is. *It's a lot of beautiful notes and sounds put together so well that we get pleasure out of hearing them ... Notes aren't about burned fingers, or space travel, or lampshades, or anything. What* are *they about? They're about music. For instance, take this little Prelude by Chopin: ... It's beautiful music. But what is about? Nothing. Or take a passage from Beethoven sonata: ... That's not* about *anything, either. Or again, a bit of jazz: ... What's it about? Nothing. They're all about nothing, but they're all fun to listen to."* (Leonard Bernstein, *Leonard Bernstein's Young People's Concerts*, Pompton Plains 2005, pp. 1-4)

that are explained in the eighth chapter, the occasion is given there to go back to this subject.

Even an author who disputes the existence of the leading tone succumbs, in a sort, to the magic of the leading tone:

"Strictly speaking, there is no leading tone, but there is a leading interval because it is not the seventh tone of the scale as such that leads to the root tone of the tonal basic chord (resp. to its octave), but merely the major basic third of the key's upper-dominant-harmony ..." [1]

When Heller brings the harmonic identity of the seventh tone of the scale into play, he does not intend to clarify that the step from the seventh to the eighth tone of the scale is a melodic *form* of the harmonic transition from the dominant to the tonic. Rather, he means that in this step lies the whole secret of that harmonic transition. To his mind, this semitone is *"the smallest interval given by nature for the tonal harmony connection that represents ... the connection path ... in the natural triad chain".* [2] Heller does not realise the logical contradiction that he gets into when he defines the semitone step equally as a *result* and *cause* of the relation between the tonic and dominant:

"That, however, also the nature wants that the differences in distance which result for the steps of the scale are understood to be distinct, she shows us by the fact that she attributes different measures for the above distances that in practice are regarded by us as equally large steps ..." [3]

The confusion by Heller is based on his interpretation of the musical aesthetics as a "gift of nature": According to this, the nature provides triads as chain links which are connected with each other by intervals, gives us, thereby, *"the musical scale and the meaning of its tones"*,[4] and, to make matters worse, places the order to appreciate its meaningful structure accordingly.

d) Alteration

The melody moves on scale degrees which are based on the tone ensemble of a key. As long as the tones belong to this tone ensemble, it moves on the degrees of the corresponding scale. However, if the key changes, then the relevant scale also changes on whose degrees the melody moves further. At the change into the new key, intervals occur that do not represent degree relations *within* a scale, but relations *between* the degrees of different scales.

---

[1] Max Paul Heller, *Die Musik als Geschenk der Natur. Betrachtungen über das wahre Wesen von Dur und Moll, sowie über die Naturgesetze ihrer Harmonik*, Berlin 1930, p. 36.

[2] Ibid., p. 36.

[3] Ibid., p. 34.

[4] Ibid., p. 32, chapter title.

The following example shows – according to the laws of modulation and of its progression forms in bars, developed in the third and fourth chapters – the first bar in A minor, the second one in C major. The interval at the bar line connects two degrees of different scales.

Interval at the transition from A minor to C major

The two scales seem to be incommensurable at first glance: The tone A lies in A minor on the first degree, in C major on the sixth. But this difference affects only the position which the tone A occupies within a scale. The keys of A minor and C major differ harmonically in their tone gender and their tonic. In the sphere of melodics, this appears as a difference in the starting point from where a musical scale with its respectively typical pattern of degree distances is formed.

The interval that connects the two scales, however, is not defined by its relation to the keynote of a scale, but by a pitch level comparison between the degrees of the alternating scales. The tones A, B, C, D, E, F lie each on the same pitch level in the keys of A minor and C major. They, therefore, also lie on the same degree – so to speak, as the melodic counterpart of the harmonic accordance between the tone ensembles of consecutive keys. The interval between the tones E and A is therefore, in A minor, in C major, and during a boundary crossing between both keys, always a fourth.

The key of A minor is nullified in the above example by the tone G. This tone lies on the degree between the tones F and A. However, the same holds also true for the tone G sharp in the first bar. Because of that, the tones G and G sharp lie exactly on the same degree. *This* degree, however, has changed after the modulation: It lies a semitone lower, that is, closer to the tone F. From a *harmonic* point of view, the tones G and G sharp belong to the tones in terms of which the tone ensembles of A minor and C major *differ*. They have nothing to do with each other. *Melodically*, they are representatives of the *same* degree. This degree is merely raised, or lowered, during the transition between the two keys, that is, it is *altered* in one direction or the other. The interval between G and G sharp is, irrespective of the pitch difference, a *prime*, more precisely: an augmented prime.

Since every scale has seven degrees with which it fills an octave space fairly evenly, every newly occurring tone of a new key basically falls on a degree that was already occupied before its occurring. The transition into a new ensemble of tones that is characteristic of the modulation appears therefore melodically as a shift of individual degree distances. The identity and order of the degrees remain intact across all modulations.

In the normal case of the modulation, the coinciding tones of the tone ensembles replacing one another lie on identical scale degrees. However, there are also exceptions to this as the following example shows:

Modulation from A minor to C minor

The tones G sharp and A flat are tones in which both of the tone ensembles of A minor and C minor coincide. From the standpoint of the harmonic perception, the different spelling of these absolutely identical sounding tones seems to be a mere caprice of the notation. This spelling, however, corresponds to the melodic reality according to which G sharp and A flat cannot lie on a common degree in the mentioned keys. This is because there is *no* further degree between G sharp and F in A minor, whereas *the tone G* lies between A flat and F in C minor. In return, the tone A flat is followed by the tone B as an *immediately* adjoining degree, whereas in A minor, the tone A lies between B and G sharp. Depending on the key, the same tones form either an augmented second or a minor third. On the basis of the alteration, not only can different tones lie on the same degree, but also the same tones can lie on different degrees (and are therefore represented by different notes).

Alteration is the form in which the scale degrees keep their identity even when changing keys. The musical notation is basically appropriate to this fact. However, the use of accidentals and natural signs is not restricted to taking into account the essence of the alteration. As already mentioned in the third chapter, writing-technically motivated breaches against the degree logic are known and usual under the term "enharmonic change". Moreover, even harmonically indifferent or atonal passages are notated in a spelling that presupposes and starts from the degrees of a scale and therefore the harmonic determinacy of the tones.

A special case of the alteration is the *chromatic* tone sequence, that is, a tone sequence with consecutive semitone steps. The tones of the chromatic tone sequence are by no means components of an entirely own, namely a chromatic scale, as is commonly believed, but tones of changing keys and their scales. An example for that is Bach's Chromatic Fugue, whose theme contains a chromatic tone sequence in which every individual tone belongs to an own harmony so that whenever the theme sounds the harmony change also occurs inside the bar. In the following two bars, the theme with the chromatic tone sequence A, B flat, B, C lies in the bass.

J. S. Bach, Chromatic Fugue (BWV 903), bars 140 and 141

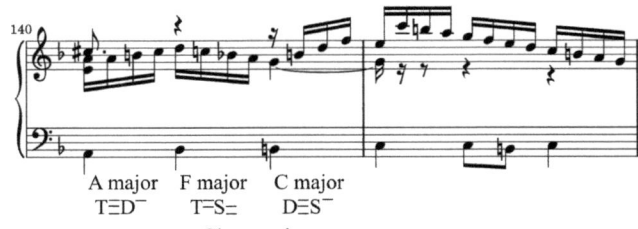

Chromatic tone sequence

In bar 140, the first third (of the bar) makes a transition from A minor (bar 139) to A major. The middle third modulates to F major and the last third to C major, where also bar 141 stays.

Of course, not every chromatic tone sequence has to feature such a markedly harmonic determinacy where every tone shows itself to be a component of a specific scale and key. Such tone sequences can also be indifferent or atonal. They can even appear in a form in which not every tone carries harmonic weight: The semitone steps can be a mere mediation of a larger tone step and have the effect of a legato. The individual tones of a chromatic sequence may then still be physically identifiable, but, for the perception, they do not appear as tones that have to be taken into account musically. Hence, they do not play any role in the harmonic assignment and can be partially unconsidered for the harmonic analysis. Whether or not there is an objective criterion applicable to all music listeners for the delimitation of cases in which the tones of the chromatic sequence carry harmonic weight or not cannot be clarified in the present analysis. Only one thing is for sure: The existence of such merely connecting tone sequences by no means justifies the hereafter discussed logical mistake of some musicologists to understand tones as representatives of supposedly actually meant tones.

e) The Construct of the Altered Chord

Music textbooks and encyclopaedias usually introduce their readers to a phenomenon which they call "altered chords" and present, for example, as follows:

*"**Altered chords**, since H. Riemann, the designation for such sounds within the functional-harmonic system in which one or more tones of an originally in-scale chord are chromatically altered ..."* [1]

The word "originally" is not meant in terms of *time* here as it would be appropriate in the case of the alteration where in the sequence of the bars a change occurs with the degrees. Rather, the quote speaks of a *logical* origin: The "in-scale chord" is supposed to be that which *underlies* the "altered chord"; it is supposed to relate to the "altered chord" approximately in the same way as the pure fifth relates to the tempered fifth. This theory does not notice that in a harmonically determined music all tones – before and after a modulation – belong to a scale anyway and are thus "in-scale". The quoted source determines the key and therefore also the process of the modulation separately from the tones of the scales, namely by a theory of harmonic functions, and refuses – with the wrong distinction of "in-scale" and "out-of-scale" chords – to accept the definition of the modulation introduced in older textbooks:

---

[1] Hans Heinrich Eggebrecht (ed.), *Riemann Musiklexikon. Sachteil*, Mainz et al. 1967, p. 32.

"What older textbooks designate as an evasion into a foreign key, as a temporary contact with another tonic, presents itself in the ... designation of harmonic function as still being in the range of the old key insofar as here the tonic of these evasion keys maintains its designation of function according to its position in the main key, and merely its satellites (...) seem to be eliminated from the old key." [1]

The construction of an altered chord allows Riemann to refer *everything* in a piece of music to the tonic of a "main key", without even knowing a single real harmonic relation. Riemann simply compares all chords with this tonic and finds that those chords, as far as they are not the tonic, then simply deviate from it. And that alone is then the whole relation to the tonic: The dominant is not entirely consonant because it is not a tonic; in the case of the dissonance, "foreign tones" are added as disturbing elements; the "altered chord" does not even abide by the tones of the "main key". All these curious "relations" to the tonic, which, encoded in countless abbreviations, make up Riemann's designations of function, just express this abstract, negative relation to the tonic and fixate aspects of the *deviation* from the tonic as the epitome of the *relatedness* to it. Riemann's naming of this procedure is quite appropriate: He is concerned with interpreting all sounds "in the sense" of a tonic.

With his "designations of function", Riemann turns against the conventional scale-degree designations for chords (by Roman numerals), with regard to which he notices that they, according to their direct literal sense, do not express harmonic facts. Now, however, the designation "seventh chord of the second degree" is quite harmless and can certainly be distinguished as a mere name from the harmonic definition of such a chord. The designations that Riemann wants to set against it are less harmless because they are, in fact, symbols for his interpretation of the harmonic connections. However, Riemann is far away from correcting any confusion between intervals and harmonic relations. On the contrary, to such confusion, he diligently contributes with his ideas about leading tones and altered chords. In the latter case, he claims in all seriousness that chords have something to do with one another harmonically due to the identity of the scale degrees on which their tones lie. Then, after all, it is more reasonable to *name* chords after degrees than to *judge* them by degrees.[2]

---

[1] Hugo Riemann, *Handbuch der Harmonielehre*, Leipzig 1918, p. 215.

[2] A more detailed analysis of Riemann's functional theory is to be found in: Franz Sauter, *Die Musikwissenschaft in Forschung und Lehre. Kritik einer bürgerlichen Wissenschaft*, Norderstedt 2010, chapter 2.

7. Counterpoint

a) Polyphony

In polyphonic music, melodies refer to each other as *voices*. Strictly speaking, the melodies only become voices by the fact that they enter into a genuinely melodic relationship: They compare themselves *as melodies* with each other, that is, they refer to each other in accordance with the way of movement peculiar to them. Each voice is constantly related in its progression to the progression of each of the other voices.

J. S. Bach, Bourrée (BWV 807)

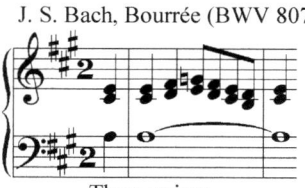

Three voices

The way in which, in this example, the two upper voices refer to each other in their motion sequence is, for obvious reasons, called parallel motion. The lower voice, however, relates to each of the two upper voices in such a way that it stagnates while those two move on. Thus, one can see, in this example, two forms in which voices can be referred to each other, and even before these and further forms are examined in more detail, a few general statements can be made about voice motion, polyphony, and counterpoint.

The melodies, as said before, turn into voices by the mutual comparison of their mode of movement. The term "voice" designates, therefore, an *aesthetic* fact in this context. That the word "voice" is also used in other meanings is irrelevant here. In the composite words "monophonic" and "polyphonic", for example, the voice is presented as something which exists independently of the melodic relation which is the subject here. That does not have to be bad, however, it shall not lead to false conclusions about the character of the polyphony.

In any case, polyphony is not just a collection of melodies that only come together externally by sounding at the same time. What characterises the voices in the polyphony is not their sheer coexistence, but the *correlation of their motions*.[1] This immanent relationship of the voices having its benchmark in the melodic form is precisely that which constitutes and defines the counterpoint. The counterpoint is the aesthetics of the polyphony, and the various motion relations

---

[1] *"In musical reality, counterpoint is the interrelationship of the voices, not their complete independence."* (Carl Dahlhaus, *Studies on the Origin of Harmonic Tonality*, trans. Robert O. Gjerdingen, Princeton 1990, p. 234). *"... not the unrelatedness* [Beziehungslosigkeit] *of the voices"*, says Dahlhaus correctly in the German original. This difference is important for the theory of counterpoint.

of the voices, which will be analysed in the following, are the forms of the counterpoint, that is, the *contrapuntal figures*.

In contrast to the general opinion, the counterpoint has nothing to do with harmony. The voices have, by nature, absolutely no harmonic relation to each other, they are not at all capable of having such a relation because of their character. What harmonises are the *tones* that sound together in bars or bar segments, not the voices as such. That the harmonising tones are components of the voices at the same time is another matter. Within a melodic tone sequence, the tones always represent scale degrees, on which, just as well, other tones can lie. The course of the voices is not being changed if an accidental is placed or cancelled before one or the other note. What changes is merely the key and the succession of harmonies. Conversely, a specific succession of harmonies can be realised in a variety of voice movements.

What is also wrong is the opinion that the counterpoint stands in a contrast to harmony as some theorists claim:

"The crux of contrapuntal theory is how two or more lines can unfold simultaneously in the most unhampered melodic development – not by means of the harmonies but despite the harmonies."[1]

The harmony of the sound combinations and of their succession does not *"hamper"* the melodics of the voice motion. In this motion, there is nothing that needs yet to be brought into accordance. The melodics of the tonal music does not at all exist independently of their harmonic basis. And also the voices themselves have no negative relation to each other. They do not stand in the way of each other, but compare themselves in regard to the form of their movement. The counterpoint is a *positive* relation of the voices.

The autonomous motion of the voices, that is, the discrete identity of the musical lines, is logically presupposed in their positive relationship. The enjoyment of the counterpoint is insofar bound to the separate perceptibility of the voices and their respective movement. This precondition is most easily ensured by performing the voices on various instruments preferably contrasting in terms of their timbre. The counterpoint and the therein presupposed independence of the voices, however, also exist in music pieces that are merely played on a piano or an organ. Why this is so, becomes quickly apparent once the forms of the counterpoint are examined more closely.

b) Parallel Motion of the Voices

The simplest form of the counterpoint is the parallel motion of the voices. In this motion, complete melodic accordance dominates: Each voice progresses at the same time, in the same direction, and by the same interval, and the interval between the simultaneously sounding tones of the voices is therefore always of

---

[1] Ernst Kurth, *Selected Writings*, ed. and trans. Lee A. Rothfarb, Cambridge et al. 2006, p. 47.

the same size. By *which* interval the voices are led in parallel motion is basically indifferent. However, the intervals differ in their suitability for the unfolding of the parallel motion of the voices, namely, on the basis of the harmonic relations that underlie the intervals.

The most inconspicuous variant of the parallel motion is the movement of the voices by the interval of an octave. This is not because of the melodic, but because of the harmonic accordance of the respective tones. Harmonically seen, the polyphony of the parallel octaves does not contribute more to the number of tones than what the individual voice already provides as the content of the bars. Additionally, the parallel octaves have something rigid about them insofar as the octaves, in contrast to the rest of the intervals, always sound at exactly the same frequency ratio, that is, the octave (2:1) has no interval variants like, for example, the third where a distinction can be made between the major (5:4), minor (6:5) or the dissonant (32:27) third. The parallel leading of the octaves can therefore also be consciously realised in a form that is still beyond the polyphony, such as in the coupling of organ stops where the upper voice is only intended to enrich the meagre sound of the lower voice, or in the case of twelve-string guitars whose sonority is achieved by four courses that are tuned in octaves. Conversely, *audible* parallel octaves can come about even without any contrapuntal intention, for example, when men and women sing in "unison". The ear gets thereby quickly accustomed to the rigid coupling of the tones so that the parallel octaves practically make themselves felt as a form of polyphony not until the transition to or from another type of the contrapuntal motion.

J. S. Bach, Toccata (BWV 565)

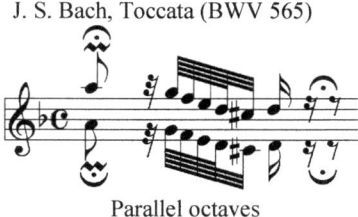

Parallel octaves

The parallel motion in other intervals is basically richer in harmonic content because they generally make more tones available to the bars. The view, however, that the harmonic content comes about *because of* the leading of the voices is a pure illusion, which can arise during composing.[1] As melodics in general, so is the voice leading in particular just the shaping of the harmonic content of the tonal music. From a harmonic point of view, it is thus, also in the case of the

---

[1] Since separate melodies can easily be thought up, quite a few people who dabble in composing resort to the method to first combine separate musical lines with each other in order to see afterwards whether the such created polyphony turns out to be harmonically acceptable. In the early stages of tonal music, this approach was even nearly inevitable as will be shown later. That theories of harmony, however, take their object as the result of a voice motion is factually inappropriate.

parallel motion of the voices, always about the interplay between the dominants and the tonic: Over all changes of the keys, the harmonic motion consists in the permanent confrontation of the dominants and its resolution into the tonic. The fact that the voice leading is just the melodic form in which the respective harmonies are placed as accented bar contents becomes apparent in the preference of thirds and sixths in a parallel motion. This is because such a voice motion can not only present dissonances, but also their resolution into a tonic which is recognisable in its tone gender (major or minor) by the presence of the tonic third. Parallel fourths and fifths, however, basically require additional voices in order to not only make audible the root tone and the fifth, but the consonance of complete major and minor triads. Even larger is the restriction in reference to the parallel motion in sevenths and seconds: By these intervals, a consonance can never be expressed. If they form the basis of a parallel motion, this will always remain a fleeting phenomenon, in which dissonances can only be accumulated, but not resolved.

Even if not all intervals are equally suitable for the parallel motion of the voices: The form of the parallel motion itself conflicts in no way with the harmonies. Even before any harmonic constellation sets limits to it, the figuration of the parallel motion itself, as will become apparent at closer examination, contains an *immanent* restriction, by which it points beyond itself at the same time.

As for the movement they carry out, the voices led in parallel motion do not differ in any way; but it is precisely for this reason that they differ all the more by the position which they occupy relatively to each other: They relate to each other as upper and lower voice. The belonging of the tones to one or the other voice is thus defined by their relative position. The melodic identity of the voices does not have to be established by the use of contrasting timbres or separately locatable sound sources, but springs – already in this simplest case of the polyphony – from the contrapuntal figure itself.

However, the same relation of motion that establishes the independence and separateness of the voices by the determinacy of their relative position also contains an element of relativisation of the melodic independence, namely, by the reciprocal dependence of the voices in terms of the course of their movement. However, the independence of the voices is by no means *"endangered"* by the parallel motion, and the view of the old counterpoint doctrines regarding this merely absolutises the, in the logic of the counterpoint, further developed shapes with which the early polyphony has been advanced.[1]

---

[1] *"While in primordial and usual polyphony, also in case of the early organum, the motion in parallel fifths or fourths forms one of the principles and a starting point of sound shaping, music teaching generally forbade open parallel octaves and fifths since the 14th century – invoking the endangered independence of the voices."* (Carl Dahlhaus and Hans Heinrich Eggebrecht (eds.), *Brockhaus Riemann Musiklexikon*, vol. 3, Mainz 1998, p. 267). What was actually enforced with the aesthetic excommunication of the parallel fifths from the early polyphony will be elucidated more fully at the end of this chapter.

c) Similar and Contrary Motion

The dependence of the voices on each other by their coupling to each other is overcome by a voice motion that proceeds by different intervals. The voices move, thereby, towards each other or they move away from each other. Insofar as the voices each move in the same direction, the difference of their motion lies only in the size of the performed intervals. This is called similar or direct motion. The contrast of the voices, however, is intensified if the voices move in opposite directions, that is, in contrary motion.

J. S. Bach, Choral (BWV 15)

Weil du vom Tod' er-stan-den bist

Similar and contrary motion

The gain in independence by a movement that brings the voices into increasing proximity or distance to each other also opens up the perspective of a voice crossing, thus going a little at the expense of the first-mentioned independence which lies in the rigid separation of the top and the bottom in the case of the parallel motion. However, a crossing of the voices can only be achieved if the voices can be identified by distinguishable sound sources. In the case of piano pieces, for example, the simultaneously sounding tones differ only in terms of their pitch so that they can only be assigned to a voice on the basis of their relative position. The perception then stays with the assumption that there are upper and lower voices.

The movement range of the counterpoint is thus limited in its second form (in the case of the proceeding by unequal intervals); the crossing of the voices succeeds in this form only under special conditions. The basis of this limitation is the simultaneous progression of the voices, to which their accordance and mutual dependence remains reduced. The disengagement of the voice from this dependence is, however, already preformed by a special variant of this synchronous movement: by the forward motion of one voice at the same tone pitch while the other one moves up or down.

J. Lennon/P. McCartney, Blackbird (1968)

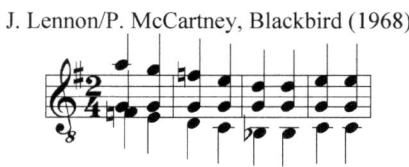

Forward motion of the middle voice at a constant tone pitch

This forward motion of the middle voice by the interval of a prime is a proceeding only in a very formal sense; from the maintenance of the tone pitch, it is not very far to the negation of the progressing which comes into effect by the contrast of a progressing voice against a stationary one. The above special form of the counterpoint is, in a less strict sense, justly named oblique motion.

d) Oblique Motion

The third figure of the counterpoint contains a rhythmic contrast of the voices: While a tone continuous to sound in the one voice, the other voice proceeds to move. The contrast in the motion ratio of the voices lies not only in the form and direction of the respective movement, but in the simultaneous taking place and not taking place of the forward motion. This is the actual form of the oblique motion (and the original meaning of the Latin name *motus obliquus*).

This asynchronous progression of the voices occurs in the most various manifestations: The hierarchical subdivision of the bar into segments can be more pronounced in the one voice than in the other one so that the voices proceed more or less sporadically or steadily at different paces. The one voice moves then further in places while the tones of the other voice still continue to sound; in all other places, the longer and shorter notes begin to sound simultaneously.

W. A. Mozart, Tempo di Minuetto (KV 15f)

Slow against fast progression

The asynchronous progression can, however, appear in very extreme variants so that the coincidence of the points in time of the forward motion remains largely or completely undone. One of these variants is based on the fact that the melodic motions of the voices are temporally shifted against one another so that syncopes continually occur alternately in each of the voices. This variant is characteristic for the following example:

Richard William Wright, Summer '68 (1970)

Voice crossing with an asynchronous progression

108

This passage, which was recorded as a brass section for a Pink Floyd studio album, contains a crossing of the two upper voices that comes about completely independently of the instrumentation. This crossing is even then still perceivable if the bars are played on an organ; because it is based on the form of the counterpoint itself: While the tone F, as a component of the "middle" voice, sounds in the first bar, the "upper" voice moves across this tone downwards. In the second bar, this voice returns – likewise across the tone F – to the upper positon.

The melodic identity of a voice is no longer bound to a relative voice position in such a motion ratio; the terms "upper voice" or "middle voice" are no longer proper criteria to identify a voice. A tone, namely, cannot lose its identity as a component of a voice during its sounding so that anything that it may interchange with simultaneously sounding tones is its *relative position*, but never its *belonging to a voice*. The autonomy of the voice motion has now, according to the logic of the counterpoint, reached a new dimension: It is no longer bound to the position of the voice, but to the tones themselves with which the voices progress.

Another form in which the third contrapuntal figure is pushed to extremes is the organ point or pedal tone: a tone that is sustained for several bars while the other voices move further. This presupposes that the consecutive harmonies all contain the same tone. This tone can go through considerable harmonic metamorphoses if sustained within the framework of extensive modulations. According to the laws of the modulation developed in the third chapter, the key of C major in the following example constitutes itself by an almost complete scale; it changes to A minor in the last third of the bar, back to C major in the second bar, and then – again in the last bar third – to D minor. The tone A sustained in the bass as an organ point begins its harmonic career accordingly as the subdominant third of C major and continues it as the tonic root tone of A minor, as the subdominant third of C major, and finally as the dominant root tone of D minor.

J. S. Bach, Prelude (BWV 569)

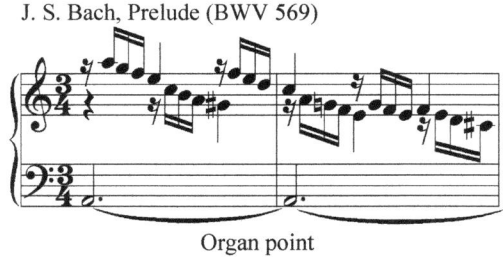

Organ point

109

e) Digression: Suspension

The theory of harmony, which emerged from the observation of the counterpoint and the movement of voices, still drags along with it its historical starting point by judging harmonic processes from a melodic perspective and thereby incorrectly explaining a whole series of phenomena. An example from the field of the oblique motion is presented here: the assertion that a tone which is usually referred to as a suspension is a "nonchord tone".

What is now a suspension really? A suspension is a tone in a dissonance that, during the subsequent transition into a consonance, moves a half or whole tone step further while the other voices remain in place. An example with the harmonic formula:

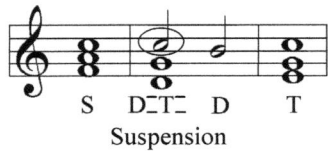

S   D⁻T⁻   D   T

Suspension

The suspension has the following harmonic, rhythmic, and melodic characteristics: From a *harmonic* point of view, the dissonance is followed by a consonance that is already partially included in the dissonance. In the above example, the dominant is included in the dissonance. From the *rhythmic* point of view, it is a harmony change within the bar. The suspension is therefore at the accentuated point. From the *melodic* point of view, it is a special form of the oblique motion. The components that the dissonance has in common with the subsequent consonance (in the above example: with the dominant) appear as tones that remain lying while the 'suspended' tone progresses (e.g. by a semitone step downwards).

A closer look at the above example reveals that the transition from the dominant dissonance to the (consonant) dominant resolves the harmonic tension that lies in the dissonance at least to the extent that it is no longer included in the *individual* sound itself. Now, the only tension left is in the *sequence* of the subdominant and dominant, which is resolved by the tonic. The dissonance is thus successively resolved.

Since the dominant was already included in the dissonance, its freeing from the 'non-dominant ingredients' appears as a reduction of the bar content to its actual harmonic core. Although the dominant is an (elegant) detour in the resolution of the dissonance into the tonic, the dissonance appears conversely as a detour in the sequence of the subdominant and dominant. This gives the impression of a retarded appearance of the dominant – or, in melodic terms, of a retardation in the movement of a voice. In harmony teachings, one often finds descriptions of this impression, which however come along as factual determinations of the suspension: This is then defined, for example, as a „*delayed or retarded entrance of a chord tone*". If the suspension is interpreted in this way, it is no longer considered to be a tone that itself is a chord tone during its sounding within the dissonance: Supposedly, this tone has no harmonic identity at all, it is simply a "nonchord tone": *"Suspensions are nonchord tones which replace the adjacent chord tone."*

This idea corresponds entirely to Riemann's theory of functions: In its harmonic art of interpretation, this theory decides about whether the tones belong to the chord that they form. The first contradiction consists in the statement that a tone, although it sounds together with other tones (= chord), supposedly does *not* belong to the chord (= ensemble of sounding tones). The second contradiction is that this tone is supposedly *not* what it is: It "replaces" another tone. Since Riemann, tones have been interpreted as placeholders, substitutes, and functionaries of other tones. In the case of the suspension, the subsequent tone is supposed to be the tone actually meant, the suspension itself its mere surrogate. According to this theory, what constitutes a suspension is its deviation from the supposedly intended tone. In the functional harmony theory, the suspension is treated quite analogously to the fiction of the altered chord criticised in the previous chapter.

e) Asynchronous Pausing

The last figure of the counterpoint consists in the juxtaposition of a sounding and a pausing voice. This form increases the contrast of the voice motions in a manner that cannot be surpassed any more. In place of the negation of the *forward motion*, on which the third form of the counterpoint is based, it puts the negation of the *sound*. Thus, the dialectic of the counterpoint has reached its end. But, at this end, the counterpoint launches a fireworks of polyphony one more time in which it repeats and summarises all its forms in a new variant.

Although the contrast between the sounding and pausing voice already shows its contrapuntal effect in the case of the sporadic or more frequent, shorter or longer pausing in one of the voices, the actual potency of this figure lies nevertheless in the special constellation in which the voices *constantly pause in turns* as this already became apparent in the case of the upper voices in the above example of the organ point:

Alternating pausing

The separation of the voices is ensured here by the phases in which both voices can be heard simultaneously. However, the movement ratio of these voices tends to separate the simultaneity of the voices into a temporal succession. This state of a *seeming monophony*, in which always only one of the voices is perceivable at each point in time, presupposes, however, the clear separation of the voice positons.

If the alternation between the appearance and the pausing of the voices occurs in a quick succession, then a quasi-simultaneity of the voices arises. These move in a similar way to such voices whose movement is not interrupted by pauses and whose movement ratios correspond to the previously discussed progression forms of the counterpoint. Hence, the polyphony is based here on the counterpoint in a double sense: The immediate sequence of the tones is about the fact that the appearance of the voices is constantly interrupted by pauses. However, once one disregards this form of the appearance of the voices and looks at the motions that the voices carry out when they each appear, then it is a matter of motions by intervals and of motion relations like parallel motion, similar motion, contrary motion or oblique motion. In the following example, the confrontation of a proceeding voice and a stationary voice (i.e. an oblique motion, or more precisely: an organ point) is clearly evident:

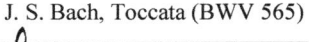

J. S. Bach, Toccata (BWV 565)

Proceeding and stationary voice

The two voices can easily be notated as *one* voice because they never sound simultaneously. That this is, nevertheless, a case of alternately pausing voices can be seen by their counterpoint. The counterpoint here is directly the cause of the polyphony. In this case, the separation of the voices takes place by their attachment to individual *bar segments*: The stationary voice appears in the above example always at the unaccented points. In a similar way are, in the following example, three voices attached to always three successive segments of a division of the bar by twelve:

J. S. Bach, Gigue (BWV 825), bar 25 and 26

Parallel motion, contrary motion, voice crossing

Here, too, the notation is simplified in that it combines *two* actual voices in *one* written voice. The two voices which appear at unaccented segments are recognisable as autonomous voices by their parallel motion of a distance in thirds and sixths. In relation to the voice proceeding on accented segments, they move by unequal intervals, namely, with the tendency of a contrary motion. The accented voice moves entirely freely through the two parallel voices downwards. The crossing of the voices here is not achieved by the contrast between the lying and progressing voice as in the oblique motion, but by the binding of the voices to bar segments. The voices thus achieve an independence by which they can move in all contrapuntal forms. On the other hand, this form of polyphony is completely dependent on the counterpoint itself, which creates the voice motion as a form of the asynchronous pausing. In this respect, the polyphony has the effect of a superstructure which instantly collapses like a house of cards when the underlying counterpoint is pulled away from under it:

J. S. Bach, Fugue (BWV 548)

Contrary motion and transition to monophony

In this fugue, the counterpoint of two diverging voices is build up only to be taken back in the third bar. This taking back already begins with the quarter notes in which, on the one hand, a continuation of the two directions of movement can still be seen, but which, on the other hand, already undo the attachment of the voices to the eighth notes. The counterpoint is completely neutralised by the downwards directed scale, which embodies a coherent melody. Here the upper and lower voice come together again and are integrated into one voice. By merely changing the arrangement of the tones, the number of voices can thus be reduced or increased, the splitting up into voices can be split up again in itself and so on. In the music of Johann S. Bach, one can frequently find examples of the construction and deconstruction of the polyphony within a tone sequence. Just as the counterpoint can vanish into a single voice, so, conversely, it can also rise again like a phoenix from the ashes.

In this respect, the fourth figure of the counterpoint differs very fundamentally from the early form of the asynchronous pausing which is known as *hocket*. The *"interspersing of two cantus with pauses in such a way 'that, if one pauses, the other does not pause, and conversely' (Franco of Cologne ...)"*,[1] as it was common since about 1200, characterises a voice motion that was not yet based on the counterpoint, but on its attachment to unmistakable sound sources. The term voice has therefore still its very original meaning in the context of the early polyphony. From the standpoint of the tonal music, whose polyphony is emancipated from the assignment of the voices to separate sound sources, the hocket appears as a form of rendering the tones of a single melody with distributed roles, where the singers alternately contribute to the melody always only one tone at a time. The separation of the "voices" is neither based on the voice position nor on the motion contrast, but solely on the audible origin of the tones. In the sense of the *modern* term voice, the hocket gives only the *semblance* of a polyphony, and this semblance disappears immediately when notes such as the following are played on the piano:

---

[1] Dahlhaus and Eggebrecht (eds.), *Brockhaus Riemann Musiklexikon*, vol. 2, p. 212.

Hocket on the two upper voices [1]

It is not surprising that the voices of the early polyphony were not determined by their movement ratio, but by the particularity of the associated sound source. A polyphony whose motion ratios equally presuppose and cause the melodic identity of the voices can only have emerged from a polyphony that was not yet based on the counterpoint for its part.

f) Primitive Counterpoint

The first forms of polyphony already emerged on the basis of musical customs rooted in magic and cultic rites, that is, on the basis of a solemn recitation according to the pattern of the psalmody.

Psalmody

The characteristic feature of this kind of music is the reciting tone (*tenor*), that is, a way of speaking which differs from the common diction by the retaining of the pitch. The voice raises and holds the tone for a while before falling off again. This monotonous singsong does not know any regulation of the tone lengths, but only a ductus based on linguistic articulation. Polyphony evolved in the holding tone style mainly in the forms of the drone principle (bourdon) and parallel fifths. In the bourdon style of the Middle Ages, a tone is constantly sustained as a *vox organalis* while, in the *vox principalis*, the same tone functions as a reciting tone or as a tone to which the melody constantly returns. In the case of the parallel fifths, the *vox organalis* proceeds a fifth or forth below the *vox principalis*, where the movement of the *initium*, *mediatio*, and *finalis* is largely carried out in parallel.

---

[1] In seculum longum, cited from: Dahlhaus and Eggebrecht (eds.), *Brockhaus Riemann Musiklexikon*, vol. 2, p. 213 (courtesy of Schott Musik International).

Parallel fifths and fourths

The drone style and the parallel fifths are the main forms of the early polyphony, which, in Europe, was called *organum*. These mostly improvised ways of music making are already documented by written records from the Early Middle Ages, but are otherwise verifiable in non-European traditions as well. The different cultures have generally created the principle of the psalmody quite independently of one another, and also independently of the scales and tonal systems each has developed.[1] In some parts of the world, this recitative music is still preserved today and is defended against "Western music" frowned upon as materialistic.

In the High Middle Ages, the style of the *discantus* emerged, a form of polyphony where progressions by unequal intervals, contrary motion, and asynchronous motion were preferred. One of the voices functioned as the *cantus firmus*, as a given, mostly known, excessively stretched out melody, while one or more additional voices – at first improvisationally – were set against it. The additional voices referred to the *cantus firmus* like *voces principales* to a constantly changing drone tone, so to speak. The voices were still fully fused with its sound source and had, *concerning the performance technique*, no *mutual* relation to one another yet: While the *cantus firmus* progressed in a quiet, undeterred, and persistent way, the additional voices were each *one-sidedly* referred to it. *In substance*, however, melodic motion relations as well as more or less harmonic sound relations were made audible. And in this respect, the coordination of the voices, which, in the cases of the drone style, the parallel fifths or monophonic choral singing, could still orientate itself towards a reciting tone and the "rhythm" of the linguistic articulation, was no longer quite so unproblematic: The musicians experimented with a polyphony whose tonal charms they did not have under control.

Occurring disharmonies seemed, in those days, to be a result of the helter-skelter singing, of which the German word "kunterbunt"[2] still testifies.[3] Against this,

---

[1] The terminology of psalmody is consciously and rightly also used in descriptions of Arabic music: *"The official style is the 'lectio' floating between exalted language and song, just as sacred texts are performed in almost all religions of high cultures. Gregorian terms also apply to this style; there is the lower starting tone (initium), the tenor and the final tone, and punctuating melismata."* (Hans Heinrich Eggebrecht (ed.), *Riemann Musiklexikon. Sachteil*, Mainz et al. 1967, p. 46)

[2] Here the Latin word *contrapunctum* has, in addition to its morphology, also changed its meaning, namely to something like higgledy-piggledy.

[3] The stylistic subtleties of this period make some sensitive aesthetes shudder even centuries later: *"These improvisations were very popular, but soon led to excesses of the most monstrous manner by adding to the two voices a third and fourth one, whereby one merely had to make sure that every voice harmonised with the cantus firmus while one did not need to have any consideration to the relation of these voices to each other.*

the early counterpoint theories created a scheduled, regulated, and reproducible coordination of the voices that was independent of the way of speaking. For this purpose, the mensural notation was created, which, with regard to the compatibility of the voices, insisted on the exact measurement of the tones. The result was a polyphony designed on paper, which increasingly did not combine *chants* with one another, but rather single *interval progressions*: "punctum contra punctum".

The early counterpoint doctrines were interested in methods to ensure a well-sounding polyphony. The approach corresponded to the medieval irrationality of a search for the philosopher's stone: The aim was to *satisfy* the ear without making it a *judge*. The innermost secrets of music were intended to be fixated by rules as if music were a question of arbitrariness or regularity. Ideas of perfect and imperfect proportions of tone lengths and sound combinations shaped the system of notation as well as the regulations according to which composing had to be done. The shorter note values were at first basically defined as a third of the longer ones – corresponding to the perfection of the number three which is authenticated in the Christian faith. Not until later, after the consecutive three-part division of the note values had already reached a certain peak, halved note values have been considered as equally acceptable.[1] In the case of the sound combinations, at first only the octave and the fifth were everywhere accepted as perfect, thirds and sixths, however, not until the end of the Middle Ages.

The lack of knowledge of the real harmonic and rhythmic basics of the music as well as the meagre results of the methodically controlled composing were compensated by claimed competence and the rigour of teaching. The assertion of the *discantus* against the further existing *organum* took place by a prohibition of the parallel fifths, *"as if it were a matter of consolidating the newly acquired by binding laws"*.[2] Nevertheless, theorists of the counterpoint regarded the principle of the psalmody as the "basis" of their musical achievements – and rightly so for the time being.[3]

After the discovery of the major and minor triads in the 16th century, the counterpoint became less important in two respects: First, the counterpoint *as a concept* received competition by the thorough bass, which made the sequence of harmonies the central point of the music composition and thereby contributed substantially to elaborate the harmonic and rhythmic basics of today's music. Secondly, the voice motion of that music became a subordinate form of the har-

---

Thereby, the combination of ecclesiastical and secular melodies with the conceivably most heterogeneous tunings sometimes led to the rarest contradictions and most tasteless creations." (Hermann Grabner, *Allgemeine Musiklehre*, Kassel 1974, p. 189)

[1] According to Pierre de la Croix at about 1300, the *longa* has three *breves*, the *breve* itself nine *semibreves*.

[2] Grabner, *Allgemeine Musiklehre*, p. 189.

[3] *"The* Summa musicae *(...) differentiates, around 1300, the psalmody style of the organum as dyaphonia basilica (Greek: βάσις) from the discantus as dyaphonia organica."* (Dahlhaus and Eggebrecht (eds.), *Brockhaus Riemann Musiklexikon*, vol. 1, p. 317)

mony sequence so that the counterpoint was carried out in comparatively simple, random, and inconspicuous forms. Not until after the establishment of the tonality and bar rhythmics did the counterpoint experience a renaissance – as the modern counterpoint of the tonal music. However, to this day, it has not lost its reputation as a (questionable) methodical miracle tool of good composing. The fact that the counterpoint in the polyphony of modern styles such as jazz and rock music is no longer named that way is insofar alright.

8. Aesthetics of the Motif

a) Concept of the Motif

The previous analysis of the melodics has shown: The essence of the melody consists in a pitch comparison which makes the harmonically and rhythmically determined tones into representatives of scale degrees and combines them in a tone sequence that moves on these scale degrees. The identity of the melody lies in a form of movement defined by intervals and proves itself in a comparison of motions that different melodies perform simultaneously. And not only that: The motion relations in which the melody turns into a voice not only *preserve* the melody's identity, but also *reproduce* and *cause* it as its very own result.

This is the basis upon which the last aesthetic principle of the tonal music is built: the principle of the melodic accordance between the phases of the voice motion. The voices take up their previously made motion in their further progression, that is, they compare themselves in regard to their motions carried out step by step, be it inside a voice, be it in the relation of the voices to each other. The crystallisation form of this comparison is the motif. By the accordance with other passages of the melodic movement, a piece of melody becomes a motif.

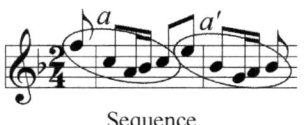

Sequence

In this example, tone sequence *a* is a motif because it is followed by a tone sequence that carries out the same melodic motion on a different scale degree. The fact that this replica *a'* shifted by one degree follows the motive *a* quite *immediately*, is characteristic of what is called a *sequence*.

In the sequence, by the way, the melody shows itself very convincingly as what it is: a progression on scale degrees that in its course is exclusively determined by the intervals in which it progresses. Relevant for the identity of the intervals is not the frequency ratio between the tones, but the number of the skipped scale degrees. The last interval in the tone sequence *a* in the above example is a *whole tone*, but a *semitone* in the tone sequence *a'*; *identical* are these intervals, however, as seconds. Accordingly, the matching of the melodic motion phases is an aesthetic that is entirely separated from the underlying harmonic and rhythmic forms of accordance.

The accordance between the melodic model and its replica does not have to be in the exact course of the melodic motion. It also exists in forms in which the movement of the motif is modified:

Melodic inversion

In the case of the inversion *a'*, the melody of the motif *a* moves in the contrary direction. A motif can be varied in its replicas in many ways: The melodic motion of the pattern can be led backwards as a so-called retrograde motion, it can reappear in longer or shorter note values, the individual tones of a motif can be split up rhythmically, and so on. The accordance between the pattern and replica, however, is generally based on the fact that, in the derived tone motion, the motif as a whole is reshaped after a uniform principle. The difference between the original and its copy, between the predefined and derived form, is usually easier to put into words than the commonality of the respective tone sequences. What is important, however, is the intuitive perceptibility of the melodic accordance, without which even the most worked out modification of a motif does not count as such. On the other hand, the perception familiar with the tonal music is quite open to motivic structures and ready to absorb every conceivable hint of a melodic accordance. The melodic comparison between the phases of the voice motion is so much immanent to musicality that a musician finds it difficult to invent a longer melody without a motif.

Melody without a motif

This example does not show any melodic accordance of the melody parts and therefore does not contain a motif. The same melody which was a motif in the previous examples loses its motivic character as soon as any form of replica fails to appear. To be a motif is a determination that a piece of melody obtains *reflexively*, that is, on the basis of its accordance with later phases of the voice motion. The motif cannot be the pattern and benchmark of the subsequent melodic movement if this movement does not absorb the pattern at the same time. Thus, the existence of the motif is inseparably linked to its resumption in the progression of the voice motion. Whether or not a motif crystallises out in the above example, depends entirely on whether and how this melody is continued and complemented. In the following example, a motif results by the addition of a lower voice that imitates the motion form of the upper voice:

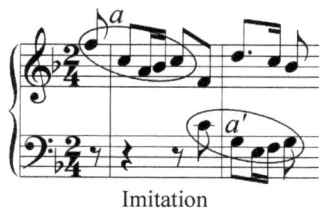

Imitation

The reproduction of the motif in another voice can already begin before the given motif has ended. This is then a stretto, in which the copy process of the pattern already begins before the pattern's completion. Many fugues begin with such a stretto according to the following scheme:

Stretto

By the way, the aesthetics of the motif and especially the imitation not only presuppose the counterpoint, but also have a certain retroactive effect on the polyphony: The melody gains, by referring to itself or by absorbing the motion of another voice, an additional consistency and autonomy, which facilitates the identification of the voices.

A comparison of the examples shows that it depends entirely on the continuation of the voice motions whether a certain tone sequence is a motif, part of a motif, or not a motif at all. The beginning and end of a motif are bound to that melodic accordance to which the motif owes its existence. A Motif starts exactly where the accordance with another melodic section begins, and ends with exactly this accordance. In the following example, the same tone sequence that has previously been presented as a motif or part of a motif comprises *two* motifs:

Repetitions[1]

Both motifs result from repetitions that follow either immediately or somewhat later. The motif and repetition coincide in their melodic content, that is, in their tones and in the order and length of these tones. However, they do not have to begin on the same bar segments, hence, they can well have rhythmic differences. In the above case, for example, motif *a*, by moving across the bar line, has

---

[1] Upper voice at Johann S. Bach, *Brandenburg Concerto* no. 2 (BWV 1047).

a stronger accentuation fall than its repetition. The rhythmic variation is even clearer in the following repetitions where the principle independence of the motif in relation to the bar segmentation can also be easily recognised.

J. Lennon/P. McCartney, A Hard Day's Night (1964), guitar solo

Motif and bar segmentation

Extensive repetitions can also be quite appealing, for example in the form of the *ostinato*, in which the permanent iteration of a tone sequence is restricted to *one* voice so that the repetitions are put into changing contrapuntal and harmonic relations by the contrasting voices.

By the way, reprises, i.e. repetitions of larger parts of a piece of music, which are usually notated with repeat signs, have nothing to do with the motif and melodics in general, but with composition forms of music pieces, such as song forms. They are characteristic for particular music styles and do not belong in a scientific representation of the general laws of the tonal music. Nevertheless, motifs can well extend across several bars, and above all it often occurs that larger motifs are composed of smaller ones. The continuation of the previously quoted voice motion from Bach's Brandenburg Concertos shows that the motifs *a* and *b* are combined to form a motif *c*:

Compound motif

To be a *compound* motif can result from the fact that a motif contains smaller motifs in its interior together with their reproductions – such as in the example above. However, a compound motif can also consist of tone sequences that have patterns or replicas outside of its own boundaries and thus become motivic components. In the following example, the motif *c* contains in itself the motif *b'*, solely by the fact that an identical tone sequence also occurs beyond the motif *c*.

J. S. Bach, Fugue (BWV 542)

Convoluted motivic relations

The quoted example is a fugue theme, and as such, it is itself a motif that is imitated in all voices. A theme is a motif that predominates in a music piece and shapes its character. Having a theme characterises pieces of music of *particular* styles, which is why the theme does not need to be "thematised" in this *general* analysis of the tonal music.

122

b) Theories About the Motif

The fact that the motivic character of a tone sequence is not based on a quality of this tone sequence is expressed by Diether de la Motte in a way that requires a specification:

"No tone sequence 'is' a motif; motivic rank is rather conferred by the subsequent, which either takes up immediately or even 'remembers' only after a few bars and then takes up, and this not only once." [1]

In order to avoid misunderstandings, one should say: Motivic *character* is "conferred" to a tone sequence "by the subsequent". This is because the determination of the motif reflects the accordance of a tone sequence with further parts of the melody, namely, as a property of this tone sequence itself, which precisely for that very reason *is* a motif. However, the common theories, which de la Motte cites in a way as if they were roughly of the same opinion, turn the matter with the motif quite upside down. They consider the replications of a tone sequence not as the reason for the existence of the motif, but, conversely, the motif as the cause of the subsequent melodics.

"The basis of the more recent motif theory is the organic conception of music according to which a piece of art grows out of small motion elements; these many times so called germs are the motifs. Marx brought this theory to bear in 1837. H. Riemann presented it in detail within the framework of his rhythmics in 1903 and gave the term the meaning that it has today in the general music theory." [2]

By the way, the characterisation of the motif as a "germ" is not a question of the *word meaning*, but a *theoretical* statement about what is called a motif. The proof, however, that a tone sequence "grows out" of another tone sequence simply cannot be produced. At most, it is understandable how this perception comes about. Adolf Bernhard Marx describes the starting point of his question as follows:

"How can we find new melodies now? – Maybe we are so lucky to have some good ideas. – However, that can mean little; we must have the certainty of always being able to form something new, must not depend on the luck of a good idea. This certainty, however, the ability for inexhaustible shaping, can only be gained from logical development." [3]

The ideal of a "logical development" is fed by the old wish of the counterpoint and composition doctrines to not only generate but even to ensure useful compositions independent of musical inventiveness, namely, by methodical knowledge and tools. The related assumption of secret rules and necessities of the melodics, to all of which one merely has to obey and correspond, obstructs the view to the

---

[1] Diether de la Motte, *Melodie*, Kassel 1993, p. 32.

[2] Ralf Noltensmeier (ed.), *Metzler Sachlexikon Musik*, Stuttgart, Weimar 1998, p. 646.

[3] Adolf Bernhard Marx, *Die Lehre von der musikalischen Komposition*, pt. 1, Leipzig 1858, p. 32.

aesthetics of musical ideas and spurs the belief of a driving force contained in the motif:

*"Such a tone shape – a group of two, three or more tones – in order to shape a larger tone series according to its model, which is, as it were, a **germ** or **shoot**, out of which the larger tone series grows, we call a **motif**..."* [1]

It may be, indeed, that a musician sometimes proceeds in such a way that he thinks up a tone sequence and then decides to let some copies of this tone sequence appear in the further course of the melody. However, his good intentions do not make a motif yet. Not until he really comes to the point to develop further-shapings and derivations from the tone sequence chosen for a motif, he brings about that melodic accordance in the voice motion in which a motif is *realised*. For Adolf Bernhard Marx, however, the motif is already present *before* a melodic replication appears. He first views it separately from what is in front of and behind it, that is, separately from the relations in which it has motivic character, hence, he reduces it to its melodic content, that is, to its existence as a mere tone sequence, which in practice becomes interesting whenever one talks about individual motifs, in other words, when it is tacitly assumed that the respective tone sequences are motifs. When he then returns to the relations that he has separated from the motif, he turns the *inner* togetherness of the motif and its replication, which is founded in the concept of the motif, into an *external* relation of the motif to its "usage", which is supposed to be something additional and the actual art:

*"But will every usable motif also be attractive, be of artistic value? – This question is ... incorrect because not the motif by itself, but the same **and** its usage determine the artistic value. Masterful movements have already emerged from seemingly the least motifs; that main motif (a) of the first movement of Beethoven's C minor symphony*

has gained and proven its full potency only by the guidance of the master hand in the service of a deep idea." [2]

From this perspective, the appreciation of a music piece is not based on the enjoyment caused by its *beauty* while listening to it, but instead on a metaphysics of a "deep idea", which – as is yet to be proven – is not entirely innocent of the incorrect understanding of the motif. The masterpiece is thereby imagined as the result of a peculiar interplay between the motif and the "master hand": The work has "emerged" from the motif, which is supposedly a "germ", but whose unfolding required the master. He, the master had to intervene so that the "potency" inherent in the motif would become perfect.

---

[1] Adolf Bernhard Marx, *Die Lehre von der musikalischen Komposition*, pt. 1, pp. 32 f.

[2] Ibid., p. 34.

When Adolf Bernhard Marx then explains how one has to handle motifs as a given material in order to get out of them what is actually already in them, he is referring to exactly those forms in which a motif can only be *realised* as such at all:

"What can be done with a motif? ... we can repeat a motif, ... shift, ... reverse, ... make smaller or enlarge it ..." [1]

Hugo Riemann develops the idea, that a tone sequence is a motif independently of its relationship to other voice motions, in a different way, namely, in the context of his explanation of the bar as *"the smallest higher unit to which several counting times come together"*.[2] He does not realise that the relation of the bar parts is based on the bar, and conceives the bar conversely as being composed of "time units" that are approximately three quarters of a second long, as he believes to have recognised from certain observations of the human perceptivity. The thus found counting times, which seem to be too abstract to himself, gain, according to his opinion, *"under all circumstances only real existence by the contents"*,[3] in which he eventually believes to recognise what constitutes motifs. The motif is thus supposed to have the function to make the time units audible:

"A musical motif, as we want to establish that term, is the musical content of a medium time unit convenient for our perception, as we have determined it as the bearer of the rhythm, thus, by no means only a rhythmic entity ... For the time being, we can ... imagine the motif as a piece of monophonic melody ... A motif is thus a melody fragment that forms for itself a smallest unit of an independent meaning of expression, the single gesture of the musical expression ..." [4]

As already the bar, also the motif is supposed to be a "smallest unit". If in rational theories something is called a smallest unit, it is usually explained in which respect, why, and of what it is the smallest unit. In the present case, however, a definition is only feigned, which already reduces itself ad absurdum by the fact that even smaller units than the supposedly smallest ones are usually already mentioned after a few sentences:

"By motif (...) one understands the smallest, independent, and characteristic melodic motion unit ... It provides the crucial motion impulse for the further course ... A motif can also be divided into two or several 'subdivision motifs' ..." [5]

"Let us get occupied ... with the smallest building block, the motif. It represents an unmistakable, characteristic, musically meaningful unity. The further events develop from it ... The motif can consist of 2 equal, similar or contrasting partial motifs." [6]

---

[1] Marx, *Die Lehre von der musikalischen Komposition*, pt. 1, pp. 34 f.

[2] See the critique of this theory in the fifth chapter, which is here only briefly summarised.

[3] Hugo Riemann, *System der musikalischen Rhythmik und Metrik*, Leipzig 1903, p. 8.

[4] Ibid., pp. 13 f.

[5] Hermann Grabner, *Allgemeine Musiklehre*, Kassel 1974, pp. 165, 167.

[6] Wieland Ziegenrücker, *Allgemeine Musiklehre*, Mainz 1982, pp. 140 f.

Also the attributes "unmistakable", "characteristic", "independent" only affirm that the motif as such is identif*able*, determin*able*, distinguish*able* from other things, but fail to provide specifications for a determination, that is, any information *by what* the motif is defined as such and *what* makes a tone sequence a motif. The effect that the motif is supposed to have on the melodic progression is accordingly mysterious.

c) Something About Categories of Reflection

The analysis of the tonal music has revealed the principle of the musical aesthetics: It consists in the fact that sound forms of the same type are put into relations in which they fit together. Accordingly, the harmonic, rhythmic, and melodic shapes hang together logically and build on one another: as sound figures that enter into relations with sound figures of the same kind, into relations in which they compare and measure themselves against each other.

1. *Consonance* is the form in which tones harmonise on the basis of their sound characteristics.
2. *Tonality* is a harmonic relation of consonances to one another.
3. In the case of the *modulation*, tone ensembles of keys compare themselves with each other.
4. In the form of *bars*, harmonies are compared in terms of their sound duration.
5. Inside the bar, the particular *bar segments* measure each other on different division levels.
6. The *melody* is a motion in which tones compare themselves according to their pitch.
7. The *counterpoint* is the form in which voices compare their form of movement against each other.
8. In the case of the *motifs*, the phases of the voice motion compare themselves with each other.

Considering this quality of the musical aesthetics, it is inevitable that the sound forms that are prepared in this way for the enjoyment of sound will either themselves represent such relations of a sonic fitting together – such as for example the consonance or tonality –, or else are correlates and referential points of such relations – such as for instance the root tone or the tonic. In the latter case, the sound shapes obtain their properties entirely from the relations to which they owe their existence. When listening directly to such sound figures, their logical basis is easily ignored so that, to a crude empiricism, a root tone appears to be just a tone, a tonic just a consonance, a motif just a tone sequence. The fact that these forms, on the other hand, nevertheless cannot be what is taken notice of as their immediate existence, makes them enigmatic and gives theorists with corresponding preferences cause to the wildest speculations. The conceptual separation of the sound forms from the relations from which they result is thereby complemented by their transfiguration to a mysterious origin of all those relations in which they are observed. Examples of such misinterpretations have already been criticised:

- A sound is a *tonic* because preceding sounds stand in a tonal relation to it. The current theories claim, conversely, that the harmonies are referred to a certain sound on principle because it is the tonic.[1]

- Harmonies take on the form of *bars* because they follow one after another in equable distances. Conversely, everybody imagines that the equable change of the harmonies is based on the fact that they are usually put into bars.

- A tone sequence is a *motif* because and as far as it is replicated in further phases of the voice motions. All the world thinks, the other way round, that a tone sequence appears in melodic replications only because it is a motif.

The principle of such delusions once attracted attention of a theorist who was concerned with a very different subject, namely, with the forms of bourgeois wealth: In the context of the analysis of the exchange value, which seems to be a mystical property of things to the participants of the market economy, Karl Marx made the following footnote:

"Such expressions of relations in general, called by Hegel reflex categories, form a very curious class. For instance, one man is king only because other men stand in the relation of subjects to him. They, on the contrary, imagine that they are subjects because he is king." [2]

Marx deals with categories of reflection whose basis he describes as *"material relations between persons and social relations between things"*,[3] and as relations that go hand in hand with fatal illusions about their quite unpleasant implications. In the spheres of the enjoyment of art, however, it is a matter of *pleasant things*, which are based in material relations between things, namely, in relations of the objects of perception, which are entirely in accordance with the properties of these objects: The fitting together of the tones rests upon their sound characteristics, the matching of the melodies upon their mode of movement, and so on. In the case of music, it can hardly have something to do with the object itself that delusions about its nature are so tenacious. But what else is the reason?

Why the current music theories cannot explain their objects, they themselves reveal at a closer look.

---

[1] See e.g. the criticism of Riemann's designations of function in chapter two and six.

[2] Karl Marx, *Capital. A Critique of Political Economy*, vol. 1, Frederick Engels (ed.), trans. Samuel Moore and Edward Aveling, New York 1967, p. 57, footnote 1. – The following translation is closer to the German text in the first sentence, less close in the third sentence: *"Determinations of reflection [*Reflexionsbestimmungen*] of this kind are altogether very curious. For instance, one man is king only because other men stand in the relation of subjects to him. They, on the other hand, imagine that they are subjects because he is king."* (Karl Marx, *Capital. A Critique of Political Economy*, vol. 1, trans. Ben Fowkes, New York 1976, p. 149, endnote 22)

[3] Marx, *Capital*, vol. 1, Frederick Engels (ed.), p. 48.

d) The Disregard of Sound Enjoyment

The theories about the motif grapple with the riddle that the motif *is* a tone sequence and yet cannot be grasped in the immediate existence of a tone sequence, the more so as it is supposed to have the mysterious ability to procreate progeny of itself from within itself. The theories in question are never at a loss for making this construct plausible. At first they interpret the motif as a musical thought:

"To a musical thought another one is opposed, the first one repeated, etc." [1]

But, what is a musical thought? *Everything* about music is something thought up, whether it is improvised or composed. So, of course, its aesthetic forms – both the musical basic shapes and the aesthetic characteristics of different musical styles – are also products of thoughts. A lover of music easily reaches the point to be interested in the musician of whose genius he has heard a sample and who possibly still has more to offer what gives pleasure. However, what he enjoys is the music, not its character as a work. In terms of the *formal* fact of the mental origin, the motif does not differ from the syncope, the harmony change, etc. Conversely, the *content* of an idea, that is, that *which* has been conceived, coincides with and is identical with the determinacy of the created object, that is, it represents, for example, either a mere tone sequence or else a pattern of melodic replications.

That, however, is precisely the point of the matter: The motif grasped as a tone sequence is supposed to be a manifestation of a thereof *separated* content, and is precisely *therefore* supposed to have an own quality. Thoughts, ideas or feelings *without* musical content are supposed to be expressed *musically* and thus obviously deserve the term *"musical thoughts"*:

"§2. The motif.

Every honestly meant beginning is worth a continuation. According to whether the same is softly-lyrical, flattering, begging or else imperiously resolute, commanding or high-spiritedly joking, innocuously dallying, gloomily pondering, painfully lamenting, etc., it will contain within itself, with a necessity which does not require any explanation, the germs of the further development in a very certain direction. First of all, the mood of which it is the expression will require a broader execution, i.e. the first task during the further-concocting of an initial idea will be the consistency in the holding on to the character, and only with the further execution can the contrasting by the expression of opposite sentiments come into question." [2]

A mood, to be exact, is not at all *expressed* in the music. It is rather the case that music in its concrete forms exhibits the most diverse features, on the basis of which it goes well with all sorts of things: with dances, film scenes, extramusical ideas, and of course emotions, feelings, sentiments, and moods. A piece of music is chosen or already composed from the point of view of such an adequacy and,

---

[1] Ziegenrücker, *Allgemeine Musiklehre*, p. 140.

[2] Hugo Riemann, *Große Kompositionslehre*, Berlin 1902, p. 41.

in some circumstances, shows a dance form, a festive event or emotional mood in the title. Of a mood expressed in a piece of music can thus actually only be talk in a figurative sense. In the above quote, however, this metaphor is taken quite literally in order to make the behaviour of a motif plausible by a supposed logic of emotions: A motif must supposedly be repeated because it expresses a sentiment that must be held on to if it is *"honestly meant"*.

The doubling of the motif into a tone sequence and an idea hidden therein is maybe suitable for illustrating the secret of the reproduction of the motif, but it does not solve the riddle of how such a motif, that, *"forms for itself a smallest unit of an autonomous meaning of expression"*,[1] can be identified. At first, Riemann develops a theory of dead intervals, with which he wants to reason the identity of a motif melodically:

"... This view, in the sense of a happening motion of the pitch, however, does not take place for the border tones of the successive, individually understood motifs, rather the intermediate interval has virtually to be defined as a dead one, e. g. in

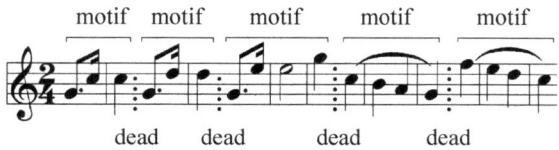

Here, I have marked the five motifs after their extents by brackets and have also explicitly indicated the dead intervals. "[2]

The statement that the boundary of the motifs by dead intervals is a really perceivable phenomenon is invalidated immediately by Riemann himself by explaining how crucial it is to *guess* the motif boundaries:

"The one example suffices to prove that the true understanding of a melody depends, in the first place, on the recognition of the motif boundaries meant by the composer. In vocal music, the text defines, with compelling force, by the individual words and by the semantic structure of the sentence, the right interpretation; in instrumental music, such extramusically defining influences are absent, and, in quite a few cases, the will of the composer has to be guessed from a number of various possibilities, whereat unfortunately very questionable mistakes cannot be excluded. In different works, I have tried (...) to show the ways to do justice to the, sometimes not clear and obvious, intentions of the composers; also in the course of the present book, there is repeatedly cause to rectify vulgar and erroneous interpretations. "[3]

According to Riemann, a composer is thus always heavily occupied to mean and say something: Already the beginning of his composition is a seriously

---

[1] Riemann, *System der musikalischen Rhythmik und Metrik*, p. 14.

[2] Ibid., pp. 14 f.

[3] Ibid., pp. 15 f.

meant sentiment, which he expresses in a melody fragment. Then, he has an opinion about where this fragment begins and where it ends. This opinion, too, he tries to express, namely by considering Riemann's theory according to which the motifs exist to fill otherwise empty time units with valuable content. Now it is the listener's task to understand music: At first he must guess where, in the composer's opinion, the motifs begin and end because it depends upon it whether he identifies the smallest units in which something is expressed, which he then also has to understand.

The premise that music must be *understood*, that something is *meant* by it, this is the basic idea according to which Riemann equally twists harmonic and melodic facts. The absurdities with which Riemann elaborates this view in his own particular way do not necessarily meet with the approval of his scientific colleagues, but this view itself does: The assumption that music is a language is a widespread opinion among musicologists. Even in colloquial musical language, the confusion between music and language has taken on a fixed form: When a conductor reports, for example, how he feels addressed by Bach's vocabulary, everyone immediately knows that he is not referring to any correspondence, but to Bach's particular way of composing. How little such speech conventions are a question of mere metaphors can be seen in the thoroughly recognised way in which music is usually defined:

"Works of music are addressed to listeners and are conceived as objects of sensually-aesthetic perception. As bearers of sense and meaning, they presuppose the understanding of the recipient." [1]

*"**Music** [...] is – within the scope of this word: in the Occident - the productive shaping of what is sounding, which, as a sound of nature and emotion, means the world and the soul in the realm of hearing in conceptless concreteness, and which, as art, by having meaning in such a way, comes to 'speech' in a spiritualised way by virtue of a materiality that is reflected and ordered by science (theory) and therefore meaningful and sensemaking."* [2]

In musicology, a way of thinking has prevailed in which the analysis of the musical aesthetics is replaced by the evocation of its usefulness and functionality for the society. Thereby, music is not simply seen as an object that is conceived, presented, and enjoyed for its own and its beauty sake, but as a means to an end. Music is supposed to calm down the nerves, revive the spirits, boost self-assurance, promote the community spirit, give guidance, console desperate persons, heal invalids, stabilise societies, etc. Modern music sociologists refer very affirmatively to all the facts where they can observe such an approach to music. They do not criticise this handling by explaining the immanent aesthetics of music, but use it as proof of the usefulness of music and the importance of their

---

[1] Gerhard Kwiatkowski et al. (eds.), *Meyers kleines Lexikon Musik*, Mannheim et al. 1986, p. 230.

[2] Carl Dahlhaus and Hans Heinrich Eggebrecht (eds.), *Brockhaus Riemann Musiklexikon*, vol. 3, Mainz 1998, p. 175.

theory, which underlines this usefulness and offers this as an explanation of the music.

In the German-speaking area, this mindset exists mainly in the firm believe that music is a form of sensemaking, which helps people in their search for meaning, brings them good news, and therefore has to be understood as a language. Accordingly, the activity of the composer is seen as a struggle for a message, and this has indeed also practical implications for composing. A number of composers cultivated the attitude of wanting to musically express something mystical and unspeakable. In fact, they have put requirements on their works and have brought standards to bear in them that have nothing to do with music and that do not even spring from an interest in beauty.[1] This pretentious demeanour has been radicalised by the methodical safeguarding of its effect on the musical aesthetics:

"The radical epoch of expressionism about 1910-1920 which is represented by Schönberg and his circle ... constitutes, by the complete break with the romantic period, a rejection of the traditional concept of beauty. With this, the negation of the euphonious triad and of its ordered functional position in the tonality are connected." [2]

The contradictory project to rebel *with* music *against* the principles of music had been put into practice by coercive rules for avoiding tonality. To that end, the artists had to know just as little about tonality as the musicologists interested in sensemaking. Grabner can therefore refer to his own false theory of the tonality when explaining the twelve-tone technique:

"In order to ensure this individual legitimation for each tone, no repetition of one of them is allowed to occur within a complex of the 12 tones, lest one tone gets an overbalance over the other and in this way attains a root tone character, whereby a tonal relation (in the sense of chapter II "Tonality" of the 3. part)

---

[1] *"The most baneful and confused notions have sprung from the attempt to define music as a kind of speech, and we may observe their practical consequences every day. Composers of feeble genius, in particular, were only too ready to denounce as false and sensual the ideal of intrinsic musical beauty, because it was beyond their reach, and to parade in its place the characteristic significance of music. Quite irrespective of Richard Wagner's operas, we often find in the most trivial instrumental compositions disconnected cadences, recitatives, &c., which interrupt the flow of the melody, and which, while startling the listener, affect to have some* deep meaning, *though in reality they only display want of beauty."* (Eduard Hanslick, *The Beautiful in Music*, trans. Gustav Cohen, London 1891, p. 95). Even though the striving for significance is not necessarily based on a lack of ability, it is, on the other hand, anything but a breeding ground for something like musicality. Further details on Hanslick's book in: Franz Sauter, *Die Musikwissenschaft in Forschung und Lehre. Kritik einer bürgerlichen Wissenschaft*, Norderstedt 2010, chapter 1.

[2] Grabner, *Allgemeine Musiklehre*, p. 146.

would be established. The essence of the twelve-tone technique, however, is atonality, that is, a complete unrelatedness to a tonal centre." [1]

Tonality, to be sure, is not based on a statistical overbalance of a tone, but on a harmonic relation between consonances which are thereby determined as a tonic, dominant, and subdominant; but the negation of the musical aesthetics is nevertheless successful. It is successful because certain musicians are more interested in the moral value of music than in its beauty, not because they know anything about the tonality that they want to avoid.

Modern musicology is so much enthusiastic about a music that acts like a confirmation of its own theoretical figments that it meanwhile treats the musical forms, from whose biased interpretation it started out, as an anachronism:

"With the dissolution of tonality at the beginning of the 20th century, consonance and dissonance lose their mutual assignment and thereby – at least in wide areas of the new music –, as concepts as such, their sense of describing musical material contexts." [2]

Would it still be allowed, after the *"dissolution of tonality"*, at least *in retrospect*, to bring the explanation of the tonal music to knowledge? If so, then the result of the present study can be summarised as follows:

Tonal music is music that is consistently and systematically shaped into an object of sound enjoyment. It has a completely and utterly aesthetic characteristic and autonomy, which it has developed and preserved against all subordination to extramusical purposes. In that respect, it differs, on the one hand, from its historical predecessors, the forms of singsong rooted in necromancy and religious service, and, on the other hand, from the obstinate attempts to become the successor of the tonal music in the name of higher values. The attribute "tonal" does not indicate a style or passing fad in music. The tonality belongs to music, like logic to thinking. The speciality of the tonal music can insofar also be summarised very briefly: *Tonal music is music sans phrase.*

---

[1] Grabner, *Allgemeine Musiklehre*, pp. 97 f.

[2] Kwiatkowski et al. (eds.), *Meyers kleines Lexikon Musik*, p. 186.

Epilogue by the Translator

After having been concerned with music theory for years, I began to realise that I had never seriously submitted the question of what is the real difference between consonance and dissonance. This was all the more surprising since I had already always found that none of the usual theories were suitable to explain this phenomenon. Then in 2010, I started asking people I thought would know the answer, and most of them, like a cousin of mine who was a student of music, gave me one of the common answers that says that it's all about the adaption of the ear that makes us distinguish euphonious sounds from less well-sounding ones. Not satisfied with the answers, I kept searching until I came across a book with the simple but telling title "Die tonale Musik". In this book, I have found a plausible explanation of the difference between consonance and dissonance. There, the distinguishing criterion of these sounds is not seen in the mere quantitative ratios, but in the tonal composition of the sounds. It has been shown that the dissonance is deduced from the consonance, that is, it is placed at a different level of the harmonising. And thereby, it was clear that the above mentioned difference does not depend on any subjective listening habits, but has an objective criterion for it.

*

In a similar way, the author's reflection on the dissonance gave the impetus for the creation of this book: In the 1970s, Max Paul Heller's use of the term *"Mischharmonie"* (mixed harmony)[1] for individual dissonances led him to the realisation that *any* difference between the consonance and dissonance is, in substance, based on the harmonic composition of a sound, and not on the associated frequency ratios, which are still used to explain this difference to this day. At this point, already during his studies in Berlin, he was certain for the first time to have discovered an error in reasoning in musicology. Closer analyses of the wrong theories about the dissonance referred him to the common mistakes in the presentation of the relation of harmonic, rhythmic, and melodic determinations of musical forms. Consequently, it became clear to him that a correct explanation of the music has not yet been worked out. In the 1980s, he found out that the harmonic, rhythmic, and melodic determinations are deducible from one another and that they can be put down into a book with eight chapters. At that time, during his activity as teacher, the course of deduction and the later structure of the book had been laid down by early outlines and drafts. But it was not until the end of

---

[1] *"Precisely in the dominant seventh chord ... we see that harmony which we can directly regard as the type of a triad-mixed-harmony* [Dreiklangs-Mischharmonie]*; ... By its very nature, the dominant seventh chord consists of the tonal upper dominant triad, which the root tone of the subdominant triad, shifted upward by two octaves, has joined ...".* (Max Paul Heller, *Die Musik als Geschenk der Natur. Betrachtungen über das wahre Wesen von Dur und Moll, sowie über die Naturgesetze ihrer Harmonik*, Berlin 1930, p. 60)

the 1990s that the author, meanwhile working as a computer scientist, found the time to write the intended book in order to then publish it in the year 2000.

*

In the German-speaking area, the book "Die tonale Musik" initially found a certain distribution mainly in Austria. This was largely due to a review in the leading Viennese daily newspaper "Die Presse". In it, the chief editor of the feuilleton, Wilhelm Sinkovicz, wrote on 17 March 2001 as follows:

"The present book ... develops – easily readable and, for all halfway musical minds, effortlessly comprehensible –, starting from the physical theory of the consonance, a coherent dramaturgy of the sense of beauty; via the question of tonality – how (and from when on) the ear can recognise and match it –, via the modulation, the rhythm – which Sauter derives from the equability of the harmonic sequences –, up to a theory of melody which explains in rare conciseness and clarity the dependence of melodic tensions on harmonic tensions. The bow stretches through to basic concepts of motivic and contrapuntal work, by which higher musical forms are only to be formed.

Not only the fact that Sauter does away with cherished and over many hundreds of years uncritically used terms such as that of the "leading tone" may cause confusion, even consternation among many colleagues. This is something Sauter will be able to cope with – because his little book will not find an antipode any time soon. The effort to refute the theses could have been undertaken long ago by those who really know better."

The last sentence of this review has remained valid to this day; because no attempt has become known to disprove the present theoretical building or even only individual theses. The established musicology has turned away from a basic explanation of musical coherences and only cultivates its pluralism of theories which, regardless of all theoretical contrasts and contradictions, are supposed to be contributions to a common concern and modestly consider themselves mere attempts, approaches, and interpretations. Accordingly, the apologetic reviews base their criticism of the book on the rejection of an in itself consistent theory of music. Typical for this is the review of a Swiss daily newspaper which considers the insistence on a systematic explanation and derivation of the musical categories to be megalomania, and the critique of musicological mistakes to be disrespect and ignorance:

"A merit of the book lies in its comprehensibility in dealing with the complex problem of 'tonality' as well as in interesting individual observations on the question of determining consonance and on the relation of harmony and bar. Sauter's gigantic interpretation claim, however, overshadows such positive approaches and makes the book, in its present form, appear as an absurdity. An absurdity, however, which far surpasses other curiosities of the music book market due to the degree of ignorance underlying it." [1]

---

[1] Stefan Brandt, Zwerg unter Riesen. Versuch über die Tonalität in der Musik, in: *Basler Zeitung*, 19 February 2002, p. 38.

The fact that his book would not be received everywhere with enthusiasm within musicology, Sauter has already assumed; and, in fact, the above review from Vienna also does contain a corresponding assessment. This has prompted Sauter all the more to drive the critique of the established musicology forward, which he has done in different ways. In the German edition of his book, which underlies the present English edition, he has criticised some theories exemplarily in an annex. However, he has spoken out against the inclusion of this annex into the English edition for two reasons: First, it concerns theories that are less known and interesting in the English-speaking area. Second, this annex turns out, in retrospect, to be a mere preparatory work to a comprehensive critique of the established musicology which Sauter published in 2010 and whose content is best summarised in the polemic blurb of this book:

"Musicology presents itself nowadays with a whole range of disciplines in which special views of music are institutionalised: Music aestheticians translate musical beauty into ideas of a senseful and meaningful order; music theoreticians construct imaginative models of such an order; music psychologists search for cognitive patterns for the explanation of the constructed structures; music sociologists give proof of the structural appropriateness of music for the social need for meaning and mental orientation; music ethnologists gain knowledge about musical order from authentic mysticism and cosmology; music historians substantiate the historically confirmed and indissoluble identity of music and sensemaking. In doing so, every musicologist assumes that his special field or even his special theory makes the crucial contribution to the explanation of the musical phenomena. However, this explanation itself is systematically – and systemically – subordinated to aspects of the cultivation of ideological worldviews and thereby unerringly missed. How far musicology has come in this respect by now, which expectations and requirements it fulfils and which it does not, is something this book wants to provide detailed information about." [1]

*

Despite insufficient knowledge of the English language, the author has made an effort to participate in this translation. He answered all questions that arose from the translation work and also tried to make the most in comprehending and checking the English text. Consequently, misunderstandings could be clarified, and difficult to understand passages of the German text could be better formulated for the English edition. Moreover, mistakes were corrected which had only been noticed during the intensive work with the text in the course of the translation. With many expressions and formulations, which are also unusual in the German language because they put new insights into words, I have consulted intensively with the author to find an appropriate translation. The scientific discussion with the author also led to a rephrasing and partial expansion of whole passages, be it in the attempt to achieve a better clarity of the presented arguments,

---

[1] Franz Sauter, *Die Musikwissenschaft in Forschung und Lehre. Kritik einer bürgerlichen Wissenschaft*, Norderstedt 2010, blurb.

or be it that the author came up with new ideas during the rethinking of the analysis in regard to how the quality of the explication could be improved by useful additions. On the occasion of such text changes, the author repeatedly expressed with satisfaction his belief that the English edition would turn out to be better than the German edition. Changes in relation to the underlying German edition of the book, if not initiated by the author himself, have at least been agreed with him.

*

In German musicology there are a few abstract terms which were very useful for the formulation of the present theory, but which are entirely unusual in the English language:

– Under the very abstract category "sound form" (Klangform), things as different as motif, bar, or dissonance can be summarised. This is important because all the sound forms discussed here have an inner connection that is based on a commonality of these sound forms: Their communality lies in their aesthetic character and thus in the fact that their components fit together. More details about this and the logical implications are summarised in the eighth chapter. In this context, the verb "to go well together" is of outstanding importance. The author therefore takes advantage of the fact that this verb can be nominalised in the German language. In English, however, the expression "the going-together of sound forms" (das Zusammenpassen von Klangformen) sounds very unusual.

– About half of the discussed sound forms are "sound combinations" (Zusammenklänge = that which sounds together). Under this abstraction, harmonies can be understood, that is, consonances and dissonances, but also disharmonies. Sound combinations can occur in completely different forms, for example as bar contents or as chords.

– The word "sound" basically stands for the German word "Klang". In German the word "Klang" is used almost only in the context of music. In the context of language, the word "Laut" is used. In English there is only the word "sound" for both terms. Thus, in this book the word "sound" usually stands for "musical sound".

– In German, harmonising means either "harmonisieren" (= bringing something into harmony) or "harmonieren" (= having a harmonious relationship). The second is always meant in this book. Because it is proven there that harmony is not something which is only added to a melody by further voices, but rather an immanent relationship which the melody already contains in itself and which is at best modified or specified by further voices. Harmony is a relationship in which the tones ultimately stand because of their sound characteristics. Unfortunately, the English language does not have such an unmistakable word as "harmonieren".

The author generally tries to use common expressions. But sometimes, it is inevitable for the advancement of science to form new terms. In this view, it should also be reasonable for the English speaking readers to get to know new terms if they really want to understand the musical aesthetics.

*

The German text quotes mainly German-speaking musicologists. If and when the quoted texts are also available in the English language, then, of course, these have been adopted verbatim into this English issue from already translated works. Most quotations, however, had to be translated, whereby I gave additional reproductions of the German original a miss. Anyone who wants to check the correct translation of the quotations can easily do this by a comparison with the German edition "Die tonale Musik".

List of Used Note Examples

Bibliography

Josef Achtélik, *Der Naturklang als Wurzel aller Harmonien. Eine aesthetische Musiktheorie in zwei Teilen*, Leipzig 1922 [23]

Siegfried Behrend, *Altdeutsche Lautenmusik für Gitarre*, Hamburg 1959 [42]

Leonard Bernstein, *Leonard Bernstein's Young People's Concerts*, Pompton Plains 2005 [97]

Ernst Bindel, *Die Zahlengrundlagen der Musik im Wandel der Zeiten*, Stuttgart 1951 [35]

Stefan Brandt, Zwerg unter Riesen. Versuch über die Tonalität in der Musik, in: *Basler Zeitung*, 19 February 2002, p. 38 [134]

Carl Dahlhaus, *Studies on the Origin of Harmonic Tonality*, trans. Robert O. Gjerdingen, Princeton 1990 [25, 27, 43, 85, 103]

Carl Dahlhaus and Hans Heinrich Eggebrecht (eds.), *Brockhaus Riemann Musiklexikon*, Mainz 1998 [38, 43, 86, 96, 106, 113, 114, 116, 130]

Hans Heinrich Eggebrecht (ed.), *Riemann Musiklexikon. Sachteil*, Mainz et al. 1967 [101, 115]

Johann Nikolaus Forkel, *Johann Sebastian Bach. His Life, Art and Work*, trans. Charles Sanford Terry, New York 1920 [85]

Hermann Grabner, *Allgemeine Musiklehre*, Kassel 1974 [23, 25, 49, 51, 60, 87, 89, 94, 95, 115, 116, 125, 131, 132]

Eduard Hanslick, *The Beautiful in Music*, trans. Gustav Cohen, London 1891 [131]

Max Paul Heller, *Die Musik als Geschenk der Natur. Betrachtungen über das wahre Wesen von Dur und Moll, sowie über die Naturgesetze ihrer Harmonik*, Berlin 1930 [98, 133]

Hermann von Helmholtz, *On the Sensations of Tone as a Physiological Basis for the Theory of Music*, trans. and notes Alexander John Ellis, London and New York 1895 [35, 36, 43]

Christoph Hempel, *Neue Allgemeine Musiklehre*, Mainz 2001 [48]

Oscar Höfling, *Physik. Lehrbuch für Unterricht und Selbststudium*, Bonn 1985 [87]

Heinrich Husmann, *Einführung in die Musikwissenschaft*, Heidelberg 1958 [15, 37]

Kurt Johnen, *Allgemeine Musiklehre*, Stuttgart 1999 [90]

Ernst Kurth, *Selected Writings*, ed. and trans. Lee A. Rothfarb, Cambridge et al. 2006 [104]

Gerhard Kwiatkowski et al. (eds.), *Meyers kleines Lexikon Musik*, Mannheim et al. 1986 [20, 37, 38, 59, 60, 96, 130, 132]

Rudolf Louis and Ludwig Thuille, *Harmonielehre*, Stuttgart 1907 [39, 97]

Gerhard Marhold, Tastatur von Tasten-Musikinstrumenten mit durch Farbe, Form oder sonstige Merkmale unterschiedenen Tasten eines Manuals, in: *Das Musikinstrument* no. 5/1986, pp. 78-79 [48]

Adolf Bernhard Marx, *Die Lehre von der musikalischen Komposition*, Leipzig 1858 [123, 124, 125]

Karl Marx, *Capital. A Critique of Political Economy*, vol. 1, Frederick Engels (ed.), trans. Samuel Moore and Edward Aveling, New York 1967 [127]

Karl Marx, *Capital. A Critique of Political Economy*, vol. 1, trans. Ben Fowkes, New York 1976 [127]

Diether de la Motte, *Melodie*, Kassel 1993 [123]

Ralf Noltensmeier (ed.), *Metzler Sachlexikon Musik*, Stuttgart and Weimar 1998 [123]

Jean-Philippe Rameau, *Traité de l'harmonie réduite à ses principes naturels*, Paris 1722 [19, 20]

Ernst Friedrich Richter, *Lehrbuch der Harmonie*, Leipzig 1886 [9]

Hugo Riemann, *Allgemeine Musiklehre*, Berlin 1918 [28]

Hugo Riemann, *Große Kompositionslehre*, Berlin 1902 [128]

Hugo Riemann, *Grundriß der Kompositionslehre*, Leipzig 1916 [62]

Hugo Riemann, *Handbuch der Harmonielehre*, Leipzig 1918 [22, 27, 28, 38, 59, 102]

Hugo Riemann, *System der musikalischen Rhythmik und Metrik*, Leipzig 1903 [87, 88, 89, 125, 129]

Franz Sauter, *Die Musikwissenschaft in Forschung und Lehre. Kritik einer bürgerlichen Wissenschaft*, Norderstedt 2010 [15, 87, 102, 131, 135]

Franz Sauter, Tonale Analyse und Suche nach reiner Stimmung, in: *neue musikzeitung* 2/1988, Ausgabe Schulmusik [58]

Johannes Schreyer, *Lehrbuch der Harmonie und der Elementarkomposition*, Leipzig 1924 [62]

Wilhelm Seidel, *Rhythmus. Eine Begriffsbestimmung*, Darmstadt 1976 [90]

Wilhelm Sinkovicz, Von der Obertonreihe kommt unser Ohr nicht los, in: *Die Presse*, 17 March 2001 [133, 134]

Carl Stumpf, *Tonpsychologie*, Leipzig 1883 [36]

Eberhard Thiel, *Sachwörterbuch der Musik*, Stuttgart 1984 [42]

Heinrich Josef Vincent, *Die Einheit in der Tonwelt*, Leipzig 1862 [7]

Martin Vogel, *Die Lehre von den Tonbeziehungen*, Bonn 1975 [7]

Erich Wolf, *Allgemeine Musiklehre*, Wiesbaden 1967 [87]

Gioseffo Zarlino, *Theorie des Tonsystems. Das 1. und 2. Buch der Istituzioni harmoniche (1573)*, trans. Michael Fend, Frankfurt am Main 1989 [22]

Wieland Ziegenrücker, *Allgemeine Musiklehre*, Mainz 1982 [89, 125, 128]